Provoc

Philosophy for Secondary School

David Birch

Edited by Peter Worley
The Philosophy Foundation
Foreword by A. C. Grayling

Crown House Publishing Limited
www.crownhouse.co.uk

First published by

Crown House Publishing Ltd
Crown Buildings, Bancyfelin, Carmarthen, Wales, SA33 5ND, UK
www.crownhouse.co.uk

© David Birch 2014, 2018
Illustrations © Tamar Levi 2014, 2018

First published 2014. Transferred to digital printing 2018.

British Library Cataloguing-in-Publication Data
A catalogue entry for this book is available
from the British Library.

Paperback Print ISBN 978-178583368-7
Hardback Print ISBN 978-184590888-1
Mobi ISBN 978-184590900-0
ePub ISBN 978-184590901-7
ePDF ISBN 978-184590902-4

Printed and bound in the UK by
T J International, Padstow, Cornwall

Acknowledgements

I would like to thank Peter Worley, not only for starting The Philosophy Foundation, but also for his continuing openness and desire to experiment. I am very grateful to Emma Worley for doing such a wonderful job of keeping the show on the road and making it all possible. Thank you to Caroline Lenton for the time and belief she invested in this growing series of books, and thank you to Tamar Levi for beautifying the book with her illustrations.

Simply by talking about what they think, my pupils at Evelyn Grace Academy in Brixton have helped me to write this book and I am thankful to them. Thank you also to Olivia, Richa and Bhavesh for our weekly conversations. And thank you to Sarah for her encouragement and her loveliness.

Foreword

In philosophy, as David Birch aptly states in his introduction to this book, no one is an expert and no one is smarter than anyone else. Philosophy is conversation, exploration, experiment (with ideas) and, in general, an effort to achieve greater understanding of whatever topic is under discussion. Everyone has a right to express a view, and the only rules are: do one's best to think clearly and honestly, listen to other points of view and bravely follow where the best arguments lead.

The exercises in this book – again with great aptness called *provocations* by their author – are designed to invite reflection and generate debate. They do both these things wonderfully well. The principles that lie behind them, set out by David Birch in his preface and introduction, are excellent. He notes that teaching should not be about handing down knowledge from on high, as a professional such as a lawyer or doctor might do for a client or patient, but instead should be a response to the student's curiosity, interest and desire to learn – and should provoke these things by being inspirational and by listening; especially by listening to students as they work out their own answers to the questions prompted in them by the world around them and their experience of it.

It is a common view, and one much acted on, that education consists in the transfer of knowledge and skills from teachers to pupils. This is indeed the case for at least part of what is involved in schooling, given that basic information and ways of handling it have to be imparted before students can become more independent as thinkers. But it is also important that students should understand how partial, incomplete and open-ended almost all enquiry is; and that in many areas of enquiry, there are no right and wrong answers, only better and worse reasons for taking this view or that, subject always to scrutiny and challenge.

Philosophy is *par excellence* the enterprise of being open and exploratory, of accepting that certainties are hard to come by and that complexities often remain after much debate. It also *par excellence* teaches the important lesson that this openness, uncertainty and incompleteness can nevertheless be highly productive, for as Paul Valery says, 'a difficulty is a light; an insurmountable difficulty is the sun'.

This book is a superb provocation to philosophy itself. The exercises challenge us to do philosophy, to think philosophically, to generate and test ideas, to try to make sense of what is at stake and to gain deeper insights. It should be in every schoolroom, and every teacher's hands, as an instrument that will transform students' interest and capacity across the whole range of not just their studies but their lives.

A. C. Grayling

Preface

During teacher training I was told by the director of the course that the relationship between a teacher and their pupil should be like that of a lawyer and their client. The idea, generously read – it is hard to shake off just how mad and dystopian it sounds – seems to be that teachers are experts and teaching is a profession, an idea which I think gets it exactly wrong, more or less. Expertise demands recognition and deference, yet adolescents are the least likely of all people to offer either. A professional teacher is a naked emperor to an incredulous audience. It is impossible to maintain the poise of expertise while spending your day with people who could care less. Composure quickly ebbs away.

The expert is the one in the white coat, unstained and uninvolved. They are never in the thick of it, never in a muddle. I doubt the course director could so easily have spoken of the relationship between a primary school or nursery teacher and a child as being like that of a lawyer and client, which makes one wonder what it is about adolescence that requires this redefinition of status. What compels us to play these parts, when teachers call for order by telling their class to 'act like professionals'? We feel it necessary to assign adolescents roles, but they are provocatively ill-defined; the thing we least want them to be is themselves (which, of course, is often the thing they least want to be; we become complicit in their self-evasion; there is perhaps something worryingly contagious about adolescence).

An expert is a coincidence of fear and need. Teachers should not think of themselves as needed (nor should they need themselves to be feared). You can only counteract the evidence to the contrary by telling yourself that you are doing what is best for your pupils, whether they know it or not. But it's very difficult to talk about knowing what's best for someone without implying that you know what's worst about them. It's very difficult to say, 'This is for your own good,' without sounding like a sadist. Necessity and punishment are cut from the same cloth.

What would education be like if we dropped the idea that it was necessary, if we didn't think of it as something we had to get right, if we weren't so worried about getting it wrong? What would we do with it if we didn't think there was any way it should be, if we thought of it as spare time?

We think of lawyers or doctors as experts because they more or less have control over their respective remits. The doctor pretty much knows the effects of administering a particular treatment; the lawyer can pretty much tell the best line of defence and the odds of success.

What is it teachers are thought to have control over? The idea, apparently, is that teachers are experts of impartation – they know how to give skills and knowledge. In other words, a teacher can control the outcomes of their teaching. So whereas the lawyer has a level of control over a bureaucratic system of justice and a doctor has a level of control over the body, the teacher has a level of control over the minds of adolescents. This, of course, just sounds silly. What we all know, but rarely acknowledge, is that you cannot teach a pupil something they don't want to learn; the managerial need for 'evidence' is the denial of this.

Learning is a matter of desire, not a question of cognition; of magnetism rather than machinery. How would teaching change if we worked on the basis that we didn't know what we were doing, if we worked not for targets but curiosity, if we thought of the classroom not as a proto-office but as the bit outside the office, the so-called real world? I suggest it may be something like philosophy.

There is nothing essentially good about doing philosophy in schools – pupils may just as well learn to surf or garden – just as there is nothing essential to, say, English or chemistry. I do not teach philosophy to impart skills, nor do I read it to acquire them (I'd rather talk of developing affinities, not abilities). I don't teach philosophy for knowledge as there is none (I'd rather give provocation than information). Without knowledge or skills what remains are the pupils themselves. The approach to education advocated in this book is one not based on teaching but listening; listening neither to console nor redeem but to crack things wide open.

Listening endows speech with reality while endowing reality with speech. Encouraging pupils to question the world helps them to see that it is something to be customised rather than complied with. By offering conversation rather than instruction, philosophy shows that the world is up for negotiation. It seeks to enlarge the inner-light, that source of shifting conviction, which moves beyond the inertia of rebellion and conformist submission into a realm of appetite, uncertain and changing.

Philosophy says it is okay to be incomplete, it is sustained by incompleteness. ('A philosophical problem', Wittgenstein wrote, 'has the form: "I don't know my way about."') It is a great leveller. The teacher may have a sense of how to get a conversation going, an idea of where the catalytic questions lie, but they don't know where the conversation might lead or how they can end it. Questions take on a life of their own. The teacher is in no position to be conclusive, the subject is predicated on mutual wonder, confusion is its currency of exchange. Philosophy is a way of relearning language.

The expert is fluent. They have little to learn. For them nothing is new. They have seen it all before, they are through with surprise. They know so much they are barely present. This cannot be the teacher's condition, for the teacher does not only teach what to learn but how to learn. The teacher is showing their pupils how to be receptive to the world, how to be open and vulnerable to its pleasures.

If learning needs incompleteness, then the one thing the know-it-all cannot teach is how to learn, for not knowing it all is something they know nothing about. That is to say, the more you know the less you can teach. If we approached education thinking less about what we should give and more what we can take, if we saw a lesson as our opportunity just as much as our pupils', schools I think would be better for it.

Contents

Jan 2022

20-3-20

There are more idols in the world than there are realities.

Friedrich Nietzsche

All that philosophy can do is to destroy idols.
And that means not creating a new one –
for instance as in 'absence of an idol'.

Ludwig Wittgenstein

Introduction

It is not instruction, but provocation, that I can receive from another soul.

Ralph Waldo Emerson

The lessons in this book are based on talking. It's a simple yet peculiarly radical approach. Children spend little class time speaking and listening to one another, yet the best (and worst) thing about school is the opportunity to make friends and discover new people. It is this aspect which is obviously the most important to the pupils.

PE and drama are the only subjects that cannot be done solo, where the class itself is internal to the lesson, where the pupils become a group rather than a random assembly of separate individuals. Philosophy is asking to join these subjects. As well as playing and performing together, it suggests we talk together. This book is made up of questions; a question is an invitation; the best questions are the questions that multiply. In philosophy the class does not take, but rather becomes, the subject. That is to say, if these lessons have a topic, it's not so much philosophy as other people.

Listening is odd. It is porous and strange. Other people's words, like their smells, are emanations we cannot remain indifferent to. To listen is to be involved, and it's to be involved without ever quite knowing what we are involved in. Though we can suppress our own thinking, it is rather more difficult to defend against the thoughts of others, to shore ourselves up against their influence; 'shut up' is never said politely. Listening opens us up to ourselves. It permits the mind to be moved in ways we cannot will. The solipsist, in other words, is a creature of habit.

Schools harp on about respect and the necessity of boundaries without also promoting the pleasures of togetherness. The emphasis is on how it can go wrong when we are with other people, not on the available goods. We need to respect in order not to hate. Other people are the enemies we mustn't make. But if that's all they are, what is the point of them? An education that isn't concerned with this question is an education palpably unconcerned with the good life.

The focus on listening dissolves the dichotomy of child-centred or teacher-led learning. It dissolves the idea of a source, an originator. Speaking and listening mixes and merges. Conversation makes a farce of supply and demand (a question is a demand that doesn't know what it wants, an answer is the supply that doesn't know what it is giving). To put the cards on the table, this book believes in liberalism without the individual and collectivism without the cult; the individual may not be sovereign, but neither should they be pressured to participate, which brings Oscar Wilde to mind. His line about the weather seems just as applicable to education: whenever people talk about it, one feels quite certain that they mean something else.

Education can serve as a distraction from social injustice – it is, among other things, the state's attempt to drum the family out of the child – and it is always at risk of utopianism, always in danger of converting our dissatisfaction with adults into a wish to create new ones (a wish that never works; the utopian teacher inevitably ends up more like Prospero to Caliban than Pygmalion to his statue).

Education, in other words, is plagued by its desired ends, which is perhaps why there are many more books on philosophy for primary school than there are for secondary. Children are believed to be more pliant than adolescents, they are pre-lapsarian, easier to bewitch; their eventual nature is still up for grabs. The effort to produce tolerant citizens, rational individuals or sceptical atheists is a race against time.

The adolescent is a lost cause; they are a kind of underclass. Though we can imagine a situation in which a child might protest that they should be treated more like a child, or an adult like an adult, it is rather more difficult to imagine an adolescent asking to be treated like an adolescent. Whatever it is about adolescents that makes adults envy them, it is not the trust and understanding they receive (these are, of course, things which the adolescent seeks to sabotage; it might be worth acknowledging that adolescents present us with impossibilities, such as the need to maintain our understanding while not forestalling their resourceful attempts to shatter it).

If we dropped that other dichotomy, the one of knowledge or skills, and approached education with an old-fashioned belief in virtue – our dispositional paths to self-actualising pleasure – we might think of the project as being to encourage, or bring out, the virtues of the pupil. When teaching children we would encourage their childhood virtues and when teaching adolescents we would seek out and inspire their adolescent virtues.

What, then, are the virtues of adolescence? Unless we are interested in this question, I would suggest, provocatively rather than prescriptively, we should not be teaching. The idea is simply that we cannot live well unless we are living as ourselves.

Of course, for us to see these adolescent dispositions as virtues we must be free to consider them as options, and aspirations, for ourselves.

Set-Up

The classroom should be arranged in whatever way will be conducive to conversation. These are three options: horseshoe, circle and desks.

Having pupils seated in a horseshoe creates the sense of a shared space where everyone can see everyone. The opening also gives you access to the board. But if you don't wish to use the board, sitting in a closed circle is often better.

The horseshoe has a leak in it. I have taught classes where their sessions were much improved simply because we sealed the leak and sat in a circle. Sitting with the class in a circle offers a greater sense of your presence. It is no good asking pupils to speak if you are not going to help them feel they are being listened to. The board can be an unhelpful distraction, even a barrier. The allure is that its filled emptiness at the end of a session will prove that something has been achieved, something has been produced. But the board will only give the teacher's version of what has been achieved or produced, and this risks becoming the party line.

If teaching philosophy were to have its sins, pre-emption and foreclosure – forms of interruption – would be cardinal. Philosophy is incorrigibly curious. To teach philosophy you need to adapt to the idea that you might not be able to identify what, if anything, was achieved. When we read a poem or eat an eclair we don't sit and wonder afterwards what we've accomplished. Profit is not the point (no philosopher ever went into it for the money). Philosophy requires you to lead with passivity.

The circle and horseshoe may not do. A class may find it too difficult to sit in a shared space. What feels communal to some will feel exposed to others. I have found that some classes are more able to enter into a session when they remain at their desks. Every class is different. There is no single way. When arranging the classroom, the question is simply: what will best enable discussion?

Find yourself a large (easy to catch), soft (obviously), colourful (exuberance is beauty) ball. This will be passed round the group, held by the speaker. The ball is like the baton in a relay. It connects speakers, it hints at a common thread. It also serves as a signal to help follow the action. And it gives the pupils a sense of security; when holding the ball they know they will have the space and time to think and talk without being interrupted or overridden. Again, some classes get along fine without a ball, and this becomes truer the smaller the class is. But, beside the point, the ball also makes the time more enjoyable. It knocks things over and hits people in the head. Pupils become rather attached to it.

If you do use the board, you should emphasise to the class that in philosophy it undergoes a metamorphosis. It's no longer an instrument of information but a medium of experimentation. I have found that if pupils are not aware of this change, they become outraged when an idea they disagree with is converted into pixels; it is seen as a kind of sanctification. In philosophy what's written on the board is not what the class is being taught, but what they are being asked to consider; the board is not performing its usual function. This also applies to the teacher's voice.

You are not using your voice to direct or dictate. When you speak in philosophy you are not telling but suggesting. So you need to suspend your certainties. The voice becomes a catalyst, a solvent. It may take the class a while to get used to this. Their voices are also being used differently. They are not reciting or speaking to please. They are speaking to find out what they believe. Speech is not a medium of consensus or conformity, of falling into line, nor is it a declaration of individuality. It's something else.

Material

The sessions feature three types of questions: *Starter Questions, Hermeneutic Questions* and *Task Questions*. Starter Questions are the prelude, they get things started; Hermeneutic Questions are the digestion, they give the class time to ponder a text; and Task Questions are the eye of the storm, the central philosophical focus. That's the idea. But, in fact, you may find that a Task Question falls flat and that a

5

Starter or Hermeneutic Question carries more energy. Don't let the book's way of carving things up distract you. Don't feel you must reach the Task Questions, or spend more time on them. The sessions are made up of several different sections and you should also feel free to skip sections or reverse their order. The book is written to be customised rather than followed.

Each session is potentially enormous. They have not been written to fit into an hour, though they have been written to fill at least an hour. One of my classes spent three hours on a Starter Question (What is nature?). We took nearly half a term on a single session. Do not feel that you must fit it all in. Somewhat absurdly, you must be prepared to change direction and improvise. Lesson plans are only for the omniscient. *deed*.

The various questions mostly have bullet-pointed questions beneath them. These constitute a map of the possible terrain, a suggestion of where the discussion may go or where you might like to take it. They are there as an additional resource. You may find that one is more interesting than its corresponding Task Question, in which case you should nudge the Task Question aside. In the discussion new and interesting questions will often emerge. If, say, you're discussing torture and a pupil asks, 'Does prison count as torture?', you might feel it'd be good to shift course and give this question to the class as their main focus. You will find yourself discussing things you hadn't anticipated. You cannot step into the same session twice.

Most of the Task Questions are closed questions, meaning they can be answered with a straight yes or no. The best reason for this is that closed questions are more inclusive. All that a closed question is asking of the pupil is whether they accept or reject something, whether they swallow or spit; it is appealing to taste rather than reason. As such, it is easier to become involved in the discussion. When a pupil has given their yes/no answer, you would then ask them why they think that, but to take a first step into the discussion they don't need to be Rodin's *Thinker*. Thinking is not an entry requirement. Once in, then you can encourage their thinking via the questions you ask.

To give the questions a different spin, you can turn them into assertions. An assertion isn't asking us what we think, it's telling us what to think, and so it can work better at provoking a response. It gives the pupils something to resist or it articulates something they believe. Rather than asking, 'Is it more pleasurable to be bad than good?', you would say, 'It is more pleasurable to be bad than good.' Rather than asking, 'Are people basically selfish?', you would say, 'Everyone is selfish.' Then you would ask, 'Does anyone believe this?'

A further option is to ask no questions at all. You may simply want to present the story, or whatever it is, ask the class if anyone has any thoughts about it, then let the discussion loose. Alternatively, once you've got the hang of philosophy, you might discard the book and present nothing.

I sometimes go in with no prepared material and begin by asking the class what they have been thinking about during the past week. Sessions that open like this tend to be more free-flowing. You might start with a thought about fortune telling and end with a discussion on make-up. A free-flowing session isn't necessarily better, it's just another option. But before you feel comfortable turning miscellaneous thoughts into evocative questions and shaping a discussion from thin air, using prepared sessions is good practice.

Every session in the book has an epigraph. I included these for my own pleasure but they can be fruitful. Writing one up on the board at the outset, you can say, for example, 'This is a line from an ancient Persian writer called Rumi. I've written it up because the questions we discuss may connect to this quote, and maybe by talking about these questions, we will get an idea of what the quote means.' Then, at opportune moments in the discussion, you can return to it: 'Does what you're saying have any connection to the Rumi quote?' or 'Does anyone now think they understand the quote?' Of course, there are no right or wrong answers to these questions. There is little design to the choice of quotes, which can make them an interesting addition to a session.

A final point about age appropriateness. Some of the sessions are quite graphic or touch on disturbing topics. I haven't recommended any lower age limits because every class is different and you are in a better position to decide what is and is not appropriate for your class. But, of course, the best way to establish their maturity is to test it – just let the class know that if anyone is finding a discussion too much, you will, without hesitation, move the lesson on to a different topic.

Discussion

The pupils need to feel free to speak. Explain to them that in philosophy no one is more intelligent than anyone else. There is no one whose thoughts are worth any more than your own. There is no one to lower our heads to, no voices that can cancel yours out. (To this end it's worth emphasising that you should not evaluate or appraise answers; before moving on to the next pupil, you can simply end with a thank you.)

Philosophy occupies a tantalising position – otherwise known as democracy – between or beyond the poles of expert knowledge and personal opinion (the task being to claim rather than explain the world). The philosopher is neither a scientist nor a shopper. It seems to me that from primary to secondary, the space beyond authoritative judgement and personal opinion starts to disappear – or rather, the ideas of authoritative judgement and personal opinion start to emerge and encircle – and requires relearning. Primary school children are less self-conscious of their ideas.

Philosophy is against self-consciousness; it is for absorption and intrigue. It won't allow us to be the centre of attention or just another face in the crowd. The meagre and the special are no good at conversation. (However, what may appear to be self-conscious inhibition could actually be a promiscuously adolescent wish to keep one's options open.)

When you first pose a question, give the class a couple of minutes to discuss it with the people round them. It would be silly to snap your fingers and expect immediate answers to the world's mysteries. Talk time gives the class the space in which their ideas can emerge. It also serves as a relief from the group discussion. Philosophy requires patience, but the risk is that a pupil will wait so long that they lose their desire to speak. Talk time gives everyone the opportunity to use their voice. As such it can also revitalise a discussion. If you notice the energy starting to flag, but you feel the present question has more to offer, you can recycle the question with another talk time.

Another important feature of talk time is that it gives you the opportunity to involve quieter pupils. By directly listening and talking to these pupils during talk time, you can then encourage them to share their ideas in the group discussion. You can reassure them that what they've said is interesting and would be a brilliant contribution. It may be that some pupils really do not want to speak and no one should feel pressured to participate. If you throw someone the ball in order to prompt a contribution, ensure you've emphasised to the class that they are free to decline. Having said that, it is, of course, very difficult to tell whether someone is resisting their desire to speak or if they'd actually rather not, so it's important to be encouraging without being forceful and to be *laissez-faire* without being negligent.

Do not rush pupils. If they lose their train of thought or fall into confused silence, give them a minute to think it through. Simply repeating the question is often helpful, but you do need to be patient and allow for silence. A philosophy session is neither a game show nor a Quaker meeting, but it's closer to a Quaker meeting. When the pupil with the ball is sitting in silence trying to figure out what they want to say, others can grow impatient and frustrated, but you need to be patient on their behalf. The concern with keeping pupils 'engaged' risks becoming a fear of their frustration. And philosophy is frustrating, just like everything else. Though we probably shouldn't intend to frustrate or bore our classes, nor should we be preoccupied with not doing so (who are we trying to convince?).

As I've said, philosophy is conversational. When pupils start philosophy they don't tend to naturally fall into a dialogue. They will give you their answer to the question but they won't connect it to other answers, as if they were all doing philosophy separately, together. So a large part of what you'll be doing is trying to engender the conversation. This can be done by asking questions like, 'Is what you're saying similar to X's idea?', 'Oh right, so would you say your thoughts are quite different to X's?', 'And what did you think about X's idea? Do you think that too?', 'Okay, let's all focus on X's question. What do we think about it?' and so on. The wish is for the class to listen to each other, to see their thoughts as part of a context, a conversation.

It can take a few weeks, it can take longer, but eventually you'll stop needing to ask these questions so often. The class will start responding to each other far more; they will start to do your job for you. It is therefore possible to be too strict about letting only the person with the ball speak. You want the class to be able to respond to each other spontaneously. You don't want them to feel that they can't address the speaker – with a question, objection or something else – without first putting up their hands. Rules are a means to an end. The best moments are when you can step back and let the conversation happen. If the conversation stops happening, if people are talking over each other and not letting others finish, then, of course, it's time to intervene. Not interrupting others is important; it's a matter of not cramping their style.

On a similar note, a common rule in philosophy is that pupils should give the reasons behind what they think. This may be a matter of temperament, but I would suggest that what you are *not* asking the pupils to do is to justify their thoughts, but rather to see where their thoughts come from and where they might lead. Justification only comes in demands. 'How would you justify that?' is tantamount to, 'You must legitimate that.' The implication is that only justified thoughts are legitimate thoughts. And we don't want exclusivity. So let's play it like this: when you ask the pupil why they think what they think, you are not asking them to reason, but to riff; you are not asking them to be justified, but curious; to see where the thought takes them and what else they might make of it.

World

'It'

The proofs of deaths are statistics
and everyone runs the risk
of being the first immortal.
Jorge Luis Borges

Imperialism and Magic

We can be competent but we are always helpless.

Adam Phillips

Until the 15th century the Americas did not exist as far as Europeans were concerned. These continents could not be found on their world maps. There was no knowledge of them.

This changed, however, when, starting with Portugal and Spain, Europeans started to explore the oceans. They discovered the Americas, Australia, and ventured further into Africa and Asia. Europe wanted to colonise the world.

It was through this imperialism that Europeans began encountering people belonging to cultures and societies seemingly very different from their own. They called these people 'savages' and their societies 'primitive'. One recurrent practice they found was magic.

In the 1920s, E. E. Evans-Pritchard, an English anthropologist, went to live with the Azande people in Central Africa to observe and document their use of magic. He found that the Azande believed that magic could be used, among other things, to make them invisible while hunting, guide the aim of a spearman, protect against witches, obtain wives, prevent rain from falling and delay the sunset.

One of their main tools in magic was a whistle, of which they had several different types. One whistle was believed to give the wearer invisibility. Another was used to seek revenge against witches or enemies. The wearer would recite a spell: 'You came to steal my spear. I am going to blow my whistle. May thunder strike you. May a leopard seize you; or a lion also. May you cut yourself with an axe. Whistle, whistle, whistle, I send you after a thief.' Then they would blow the whistle and continue, 'O whistle! O whistle! O whistle! May he cut his food on a large stump of wood.'

The Azande didn't only use whistles. If they were travelling home late in the day and did not want to be caught in darkness, they would place a stone in a tree in order to delay the sunset, saying, 'You, stone, may the sun not be quick to fall today.' Stones would also be used to stop the rain during the construction of buildings or huts, or on the day of a feast. The stone would be hung in the air accompanied with these words, 'May rain not fall, when rain appears as though it is about to fall may it remain firm like the stone.'

Starter Question   Do you think their magic worked?

Questions to take you further

❖ Is it appropriate to speak of magic as working?

❖ Is magic practical? Is performing rain magic an alternative to buying an umbrella?

❖ Why would the Azande practice magic if it weren't successful?

Having observed such practices, many Europeans believed that these societies were not as progressed as their own. They believed that these peoples used magic because they didn't yet know how nature really worked. These Europeans were certain that magic was false and that its practice revealed the undeveloped minds of primitive people. They saw magic as a kind of science, but a science based on a wildly incorrect understanding of nature and the forces that govern it.

Task Question 1   Is magic primitive?

Questions to take you further

❖ Is magic bad science?

❖ Is it possible for us to understand the Azande's practices?

❖ Does science show us how nature really works?

❖ Do those who practice magic have undeveloped minds? Are they less advanced than us?

❖ Could science and magic coexist within a single culture?

❖ Is there anything wrong with being primitive?

❖ Do we have our own forms of magic?

❖ Can we live without myth, religion or superstition?

❖ What is magic? Is it an acknowledgement or a denial of human helplessness?

Imagine that Evans-Pritchard felt he ought to help the Azande. Though he respected their customs and their way of life, he believed their lives could be improved. For example, if he replaced their magic with medicine, their lives would be longer and healthier. He could establish a school in order to teach the children and adults about the discoveries of science, build a hospital and introduce technology into their society.

Task Question 2   Should he do this?

Questions to take you further

❖ Do they need educating?

❖ Do their lives need improving?

❖ What things make a life better?

❖ Can we know what's best for other people?

❖ Are some cultures superior to others?

❖ Should he also build a church in order to save their souls?

❖ Is introducing them to his religion like introducing them to science?

Madness

Sanity is a madness put to good uses; waking life is a dream controlled.

George Santayana

1. This man was a doctor who killed over 250 of his patients. His victims were mostly elderly men and women. They were killed by being injected with a drug called diamorphine. The doctor would report that they had died of natural causes. The murders took place over the course of 23 years but aroused little suspicion. He ran his own practice and was highly dedicated to his work. His colleagues believed he was an excellent doctor. His patients said that he was friendly and reliable. When he was arrested for murder they couldn't believe it, they thought it had to be a mistake.

    This is a description of Harold Shipman, Britain's most prolific serial killer. Following an inquiry, psychiatrists found no indications of 'mental illness'.

2. This woman belonged to a violent and dangerous gang. She was feared and trusted no one. But her life completely changed. Here she explains how: 'One morning when I was walking home I heard a voice from the sky calling my name. I looked up and saw that the sun was talking to me. It had the voice of an old German lady. She said, "You are slowly dying." I asked her, "What do you mean?", but she vanished and the sky turned black. I collapsed to the floor and woke up blind. For three days I could not see. When my sight returned I began a new life.' Following this experience the woman left the gang and gave herself a new name. She started working for a charity that helps ex-prisoners

return to ordinary life. She still talks to the sun, and the sun, she claims, still talks back.

This is an adaptation of St Paul's conversion.

3. He works for a powerful company. His day is spent looking at numbers. The sole aim of his job is to make as much money as possible. He works 14 hours a day. Sometimes he can barely conceive of a world outside his office. His work exhausts him. He often thinks of leaving but the company pays well and he wants to expand his wealth. When he goes to sleep at night he dreams of numbers on computer screens. On at least a couple of occasions he has missed a family member's funeral in order to work. He hardly sees his wife and two children, but when he's at work he doesn't miss anyone. At work his mind is solely on money.

This is drawn from personal accounts given in The Guardian's *'Banking Blog'.*

Starter Question 1   Which, if any, of these three people are mad?

Questions to take you further

❖ Which is in need of help?

❖ What sort of help is required?

Take each of the cases in turn. As the pupils are expressing their thoughts on which is mad, board their reasons for thinking so. This way you'll build up a map of answers addressing the implicit question:

Starter Question 2   What is madness?

A thing is delineated by what it is not, so with 'What is … ' questions it is useful to look for opposites, to ask what the opposite of madness is – what sanity is – and how close we can come to madness without actually being mad. Things are also delineated by the values we place on them, by the tenor of our fears and desires towards them. So you might additionally ask, 'Is it good to be mad? Is madness something we should be striving for?'

Shakespeare's play *Macbeth* is a story of murder and guilt. Macbeth and his wife, Lady Macbeth, plot to murder the king and take his throne. Macbeth has his doubts but Lady Macbeth is insistent. While the king is in bed, Macbeth kills him with a dagger. Lady Macbeth places the bloody weapon beside the king's sleeping servants in order to implicate them. She commands Macbeth to wash his hands: 'A little water clears us of this deed.' Macbeth is crowned the new king.

The Macbeths, however, are not comfortable in their new lives, with their new power. Macbeth, fearing that he will himself be dethroned, orders a wave of deaths. Late in the play Lady Macbeth is seen shuffling through the night talking to herself. Her maid fetches the doctor. Lady Macbeth is not aware of them, she sees no one else. She washes her hands to cleanse them of blood, but neither her maid nor her doctor can see any blood there.

Doct. What is it she does now? Look how she rubs her hands.

Gent. It is an accustom'd action with her. I have known her continue in this a quarter of an hour.

Lady M. Yet here's a spot.

Doct. Hark! she speaks.

Lady M. Out, damned spot! out, I say! – Hell is murky – Who would have thought the old man to have so much blood in him? Here's the smell of blood still: all the perfumes of Arabia will not sweeten this little hand. Oh! oh! oh!

Doct. This disease is beyond my practice.

To get a better feel of the character and the scene, it would be helpful to show a clip from a film adaptation; Polanski's, for example.

Hermeneutic Question 1   Could Lady Macbeth see blood on her hands?

Questions to take you further

- Was there blood on Lady Macbeth's hands?

- If perceiving blood is a way of perceiving guilt, does that mean she perceives something real?

- Can perceiving blood be a way of perceiving guilt?

- There is no blood on her hands in the film. Is the film showing us things as they really are or can it only show a particular perspective?

This question could be read as trivial: 'Of course she can see blood on her hands, that's why she's washing them.' To take this answer into philosophy, you could pursue a dialogue along the following lines:
'Could the doctor see blood?'
'No.'
'Why?'
'Because there wasn't any.'
'So Lady Macbeth could see something that wasn't there?'
'Yes.'
'So was she seeing it or imagining it?'
'Imagining it.'
'Is it impossible, then, to see something that isn't there?'

Hermeneutic Question 2   Was Lady Macbeth mad?

Questions to take you further

❖ Was she detached from reality?

❖ Can we make sense of her behaviour?

❖ Was she abnormal?

❖ What would be the sane thing to do in her circumstances?

Task Question 1   If only you can see something, does that mean it isn't real?

Questions to take you further

❖ How can we establish what is real?

❖ What does it mean to say that something is real?

❖ Is what is real the same for everyone?

❖ Are hallucinations a sign of madness?

❖ What are hallucinations? What is seeing?

❖ Is it a sign of madness to believe in something that isn't real?

In 1955 the German philosopher Erich Fromm published *The Sane Society*, a book which diagnosed whole societies as mad. He believed that the obsession with money and profit found in Western capitalist societies was symptomatic of a grand scale mental illness. Capitalism leaves people alienated and alienation is madness.

Mental health is characterized by the ability to love and to create. The aim of life is to live it intensely, to be fully born, to be fully awake. The mentally healthy person is the person who lives by love, reason and faith, who respects life, his own and that of his fellow man.

Alienation is a mode of experience in which the person experiences himself as an alien. He does not experience himself as the center of his world, as the creator of his own acts – but his acts have become his masters, whom he obeys. The alienated person is out of touch with himself as he is out of touch with any other person. The alienated person cannot be healthy. He is lacking in a sense of self. Alienated man is unhappy. He is glad to have finished another day without failure or humiliation, rather than to greet the new day with the enthusiasm which only the 'I am I' experience can give.

Hermeneutic Question 3   What does Fromm mean by 'alienation'?

Questions to take you further

* Do you experience yourself as the centre of your world?

* Do you agree with his characterisation of mental health?

* Is good mental health the same thing as sanity?

* Should we try to be as healthy as we can be? Is it possible to be too healthy?

* Do you agree with his account of the aims of life?

* How can we find out what the aims of life are?

* Does his diagnosis sound correct? Can you see this alienation within our society?

To help pupils understand and respond to Fromm, it can be useful to apply his mental health criteria to the case studies at the beginning of the session: 'Which of these three would Fromm diagnose as mentally healthy? Is he right? And what would he say about Lady Macbeth?'

In defence of his claim that society is mad, Fromm wrote: 'The fact that millions of people share the same vices does not make these vices virtues, the fact that they share so many errors does not make the errors to be truths, and the fact that millions of people share the same forms of mental pathology does not make these people sane.'

Task Question 2   Can a whole society be mad?

Questions to take you further

* Is sanity just a matter of fitting in?

* Is our society mad?

* If society is mad, does that mean that each individual within it is mad?

* If everyone can see something, does that mean it has to be real?

* Can the mad cure themselves? If society is mad, who can cure it?

Time

In nature every moment is new; the past is always swallowed and forgotten; the coming only is sacred.

Ralph Waldo Emerson

Greek, biblical and Roman stories of the world's creation say that before there was earth and sea and stars, all that existed was chaos, a dark formless void. They describe the emergence of land and light; the making and shaping of humans from clay or dust. But they do not describe the creation of time.

The elements were disentangled and the earth was moulded. Sleep, Dreams and Joy were the children of Night and Erebus (darkness). The first creatures – Cyclopes and Titans – were the children of Earth and Sky. Our life and soul began with a breath from God.

These stories recount the origins of day and night, darkness and light, life and death. Yet the origin of time goes unmentioned.

Hermeneutic Question 1   Why don't these creation stories describe the creation of time?

Questions to take you further

❖ Is time an inseparable aspect of all things rather than a distinct ingredient?

❖ Is time essentially related to one of the things mentioned? (Analogously, if it were said that mountains were made, it would not need to be said that valleys were made; mountains and valleys go together, they are essentially related.)

❖ Would it have been possible to have created everything else except time? Is a timeless world possible?

❖ In your creation myth, how would you describe the creation of time?

Starter Question 1   What is time?

Questions to take you further

❖ Is it a force?

❖ Is it an object?

❖ Is it inside us? Is it outside us?

❖ Can it be escaped?

❖ Is it something private or something shared?

- ❖ Does everything in the world age?

- ❖ If you destroyed all clocks, would you have destroyed time?

- ❖ If you destroyed the sun, would you have destroyed time?

- ❖ What would you have to destroy to destroy time?

For hundreds of years those wanting to know the future turned to the writings of Nostradamus.

Nostradamus was born in France in 1503 and worked as a healer, creating his own herbal remedies to cure the sick; some of these remedies he used on victims of the plague. He had many different interests, publishing books on how to make jam, love potions and mouthwash. But it is for his prophecies that he is remembered.

These prophecies were written as poems, divided into verses of four lines, called quatrains. Through his visions and study of the stars, Nostradamus tried to map, in a thousand quatrains, the future history of the world, up to the year 3737.

Many believe he was successful. For example, Nostradamus wrote:

The blood of the just will commit a fault at London,
Burnt through lightning of twenty threes the six:
The Ancient Lady will fall from her high place,
Several of the same sect will be killed.

The quatrain seems to describe an event in London that will burn and kill many people. The second line suggests this will occur in the year 'twenty threes the six'. Twenty multiplied by three gives sixty, and adding 'the six', that makes 66. And in the year 1666, a small fire that started in a bakery in London grew, and spread, and blazed for three days, destroying thousands of homes.

Nostradamus is also credited with having foreseen the rise of Napoleon 200 years prior to the fact. In one quatrain he wrote, 'PAU, NAY, LORON will be more fire than of blood.' Rearranging the letters, the line reads, 'NAPAULON ROY will be more fire than of blood.' *Roi* is French for 'king', suggesting that 'NAPAULON ROY' means Napaulon – or Napoleon – the king. Moreover, Napoleon wasn't royalty, he was a soldier. His reign was established through fire power rather than family, he was 'more fire than of blood'.

Elsewhere Nostradamus wrote:

From simple soldier he will attain to empire,
From short robe he will attain to long:
Valiant in arms in the Church the very worst,
To vex the priests as water does the sponge.

Napoleon rose from a soldier to an emperor and he opposed the Catholic Church, imprisoning the pope and granting religious freedom to the Catholic lands he conquered.

Nostradamus is believed to have prophesied the influence of another megalomaniac. Consider these quatrains:

From the very depths of the West of Europe
A young child will be born of poor people
He who by his tongue will seduce a great troop
His fame will increase towards the realm of the East.

Beasts ferocious with hunger will cross the rivers,

The greater part of the battlefield will be against Hister.

Into a cage of iron will the great one be drawn,

When the child of Germany obeys no law.

Hermeneutic Question 2   What could these verses be interpreted as predicting?

Questions to take you further

❖ Is there such a thing as a wrong interpretation? If not, can there be a right one?

❖ Can meaning be found in anything? Does everything mean something?

❖ Is it possible to know whether we are finding meaning or making it up?

❖ What is meaning?

If you wanted to fork into a discussion of the final bullet point, you could frame it like this: write 'nose' on the board and ask what it means, then draw a squiggle and ask what that means. If the squiggle is said to mean nothing, ask why one collection of lines on the board has meaning while the other does not. What's the big difference? What's responsible for the difference?

Approximately 300 years after Nostradamus wrote the preceding quatrain, Hitler was born in Western Europe to poor parents. He used powerful speeches – his skill with his tongue – to dazzle and rule over Germany. In the East, Japan became his ally. But the 'greater part' of the world was against him.

The following quatrain has been interpreted as predicting an event which has not yet happened:

Mabus then will soon die, there will come
A dreadful destruction of people and animals.
Suddenly there will be vengeance,
One hundred hands, thirst and hunger, when the comet passes.

This time of 'dreadful destruction' could be read as predicting the end of the world. If we identify the mentioned comet as Halley's Comet, it follows that the end will come the next time she passes Earth: 2061. Maybe only then will we find out who Mabus is.

Starter Question 2   Do you think the world will end someday?

Questions to take you further

❖ Could the world last forever?

❖ Is anything in the world permanent?

❖ Do all things come to an end?

❖ Are some things inevitable?

❖ What does 'the end of the world' mean? What would remain after it is gone?

This question can be taken empirically as well as philosophically. The evidence suggests that the Earth will be consumed by the sun in a few billion years, but you can take this empirical answer philosophically by seeing whether it corresponds to a wider metaphysical worldview. For example, you might follow such an answer with the question, 'Is there anything that lasts forever? Is there a kind of law that says everything must come to an end?'

The follow-up question might seem too complicated to ask off the cuff, but sometimes the unpredictability of our spontaneous thoughts can be fruitful. If pupils seem at a loss with the follow-up, simply move on.

Task Question 1   Did Nostradamus know the future?

Questions to take you further

* Is it possible to know the future?

* Do you *know* what you'll do tomorrow?

* If we don't know the future, is it because we aren't clever enough?

* Can we only have knowledge of things we've experienced?

* Does knowing that Saturday will come after Friday mean that we know the future?

* If you buy a lottery ticket and say, 'I just know these are the correct numbers,' and it turns out you are right, does that mean you did know the numbers?

Task Question 2   Does the future exist?

Questions to take you further

* If it exists, where is it?

* Imagine someone stopped you and said, 'I'm looking for the past. Where can I find it?' What would you tell them? And what if they said they were looking for the future?

* Can you see the past in this room? Can you see the future in this room?

* 'If the future exists, and in the future you have children, it follows that your children exist.' Is this correct?

* Have the future events of your life already been decided? Who decided them?

- If the future does exist, can we change it?
- If the future does exist, are we free?
- Does the past exist?
- Is only the present real?

The Argentine writer Jorge Luis Borges once wrote a poem called 'Someone' which contains these lines:

---

the proofs of death are statistics
and everyone runs the risk
of being the first immortal.

Task Question 3   Is this true? Are you possibly the first immortal?

Questions to take you further

- Do we know we will die? Is this a certainty?
- Do all living things die?
- Is time responsible for death?
- What do you think 'the proofs of death are statistics' means?
- How do we know that death happens?
- Why do you think Borges calls the possibility of immortality a risk?

Art and Reality

How can we know the dancer from the dance?

W. B. Yeats

This session is based around Marcel Duchamp's Fountain *and Jackson Pollock's* Lavender Mist. *Because these pieces will be considered as game changers, it would be helpful to start by using the board to present a context of canonised art, e.g. Botticelli's* Primavera, *Da Vinci's* Mona Lisa, *Brueghel's* Hunters in the Snow, *Velázquez's* Las Meninas, *Caravaggio's* The Incredulity of Saint Thomas, *Turner's* Mortlake Terrace, *Renoir's* The Boating Party Lunch.

In 1917 the American Society of Independent Artists advertised its wish to hold an exhibition in New York that would showcase the latest in contemporary art. There would be no jury and no prizes, simply the work. The only requirement for an artist wanting to exhibit was the payment of a small fee.

Marcel Duchamp, a Frenchman who was a director at the Society, decided to submit a piece. He visited a plumber's merchant, bought a urinal (cue picture), signed it 'R Mutt 1917' and, with a made-up address, sent it pseudonymously to the Society, but they refused to exhibit it.

Contradicting the claim that there would be no jury, the board of directors, some of whom were outraged by the urinal (known as *Fountain*), had met to deliberate on whether it should be rejected. Though it was highlighted that the entrance fee – the only requirement – had been paid, a slim majority ultimately voted against its inclusion on the grounds that it was indecent and it wasn't art. Duchamp, without letting on that *Fountain* was his, resigned from the Society.

Task Question 1   Is *Fountain* art?

Questions to take you further

❖ Is *Fountain* indecent?

❖ Can something indecent be art? (Consider Bronzino's *An Allegory with Venus and Cupid* or Caravaggio's *The Incredulity of St Thomas* for that matter.)

❖ Should art be virtuous? Should it be good for us?

❖ Should art be pleasurable?

❖ Did Duchamp create *Fountain*? Is he the artist?

❖ At what point did it become art? When it was first made? Signed? Submitted? Rejected?

❖ Are urinals art?

❖ Should the government use taxpayers' money to exhibit urinals (as it does at Tate Modern)?

Three decades after Duchamp's *Fountain*, *Life* magazine – a hugely popular periodical in the US – featured a piece on the artist Jackson Pollock entitled, 'Is he the greatest living painter in the United States?'

Shirking the brushstroke, Pollock made his paintings by pouring, dripping and flicking paint onto a canvas laid out on the floor, using sticks and dried-out brushes as his tools (cue picture). Like Duchamp, his work was met with hostility and derision. The magazine received over

500 letters in response to the article. Only a few were positive. Most took the tone of those art critics who had described Pollock's paintings as a 'mop of tangled hair' and a sign of the 'disintegration' of modern painting.

Task Question 2   Is *Lavender Mist* art?

Questions to take you further

* Should artists be highly skilled? Is art a skill?

* Should art have a clear meaning?

* Are there any limits to what art can be?

* What does it mean to call something 'art'? Does that word change the way we look at an object? Does it change the value of an object?

* If *Lavender Mist* and *Fountain* are both art, what is it they have in common?

* Is *Lavender Mist* a good picture?

Pupils may say that it isn't art because it is awful. Here you might ask why it isn't just awful art rather than pseudo-art (a leaky bucket is still a bucket). What does art need that Lavender Mist *lacks? Can art be awful or is it necessarily good?*

If it is said that the painting is just a mess, the underlying idea may be that a mess is meaningless and art ought to be meaningful. (Can mess be meaningful? What is mess? What is wrong with meaninglessness?) However, pupils will not often be conscious of their underlying ideas, so if you ask, 'Why can't art be messy?', and they respond with, 'Because art's supposed to be skilful and there's nothing skilful about making a mess,' on a hunch you might then ask, 'And do you think that art has to be meaningful?' If they say no or look confused, you can simply return to their original idea; if they say, 'Yes! Art has to be something you can make sense of,' then your question has worked as a catalyst to their own thoughts.

Suggestion is not indoctrination, and fear of the latter can lead to a neglect of the former. It is good and valuable to propose and provoke ideas – do not worry about influencing the thoughts of the pupils. Such worry is the neurosis of liberalism, to put it technically.

Clement Greenberg, a New York art critic of the time, declared Pollock, 'the most powerful painter in contemporary America', and others eventually cottoned on; Pollock is now a standard fixture in lists of great 20th century artists. Greenberg claimed that his paintings were so vital and new because they weren't about anything, they weren't pretending to be something other than what they were.

Painters of the past, the 'Old Masters', had tried to make what looked like three-dimensional images, but this was an illusion, a trick of perspective. Pollock's paintings were different. They weren't representations of the world. They were simply and purely lines of paint on a flat canvas. They were about nothing other than themselves.

Task Question 3   Does *Lavender Mist* depict reality?

Questions to take you further

❖ Does it depict objects? Must a depiction of reality include a depiction of objects?

❖ Do emotions and moods represent reality? Is reality moody?

❖ Is art separate from reality?

❖ Can a painting be more real than a photograph?

❖ If art depicts reality, why not just look at reality? Why make art?

❖ Does music depict reality?

❖ What is reality?

It's been suggested in a few sessions that the painting depicts a satellite's view of London, which is kind of interesting when you think about it, and here you could spin off into a discussion on whether London is a splattered complex of startling chaos, a place you cannot completely live in without also living above, as though you are always both inside and vertiginously detached; but you could also look at the authority of an artist's intentions. For example, 'If Pollock didn't intend it to be a picture of London, is it wrong to say it is a picture of London?', 'If Van Gogh told us that his vase of sunflowers was actually an alien sea-creature, would it be wrong to maintain that it is a vase of sunflowers?', 'If Pollock confessed that he was feeling sleepy when he made the painting, would it be wrong to say that it is an exuberant expression of freedom?' and so on.

Belief in God

Our faculties of belief were not primarily given us to make orthodoxies and heresies withal; they were given us to live by.

William James

Richard Dawkins became famous for his writings on evolutionary biology, but he is now mostly known for his views on religion. His most popular book, *The God Delusion,* has sold over 2 millions copies. In it he argues that God is a fantasy. Dawkins is proud of his atheism; he believes it is indicative of a healthy mind.

This is a sample of his critique of religious belief:

If anybody wants to believe in things like God or the Easter Bunny or the Tooth Fairy, it's up to them to provide the evidence for it.

Human minds, in general, are brought up to believe that faith is a virtue, that you don't have to have evidence for something, that you can positively retreat behind faith and say, 'Don't ask me about that, you've no right to ask me. That's my faith. It's private. It's mine. I believe it and you've got to respect it.'

Well I don't respect it. What I respect are beliefs that are based on evidence.

Dawkins' comments are likely to offend some. It would be good to give the offended the opportunity to vent their anger before going on to focus on the Task Question. You can begin by simply asking, 'What do you think of what he says?'

Task Question 1   Is believing in God like believing in the Tooth Fairy?

Questions to take you further

* Does believing in God require evidence?

* What counts as evidence?

* Do we have the right to believe whatever we like?

* Is faith a virtue?

* Should we always respect other people's beliefs?

If God is a fiction, perhaps it is wrong for parents to raise their children to believe in Him, to subject their children's minds to fantasy and delusion. Dawkins thinks so:

I do not think that children should be told when they're too young to understand, 'You are a Catholic child, this is what you believe.' That I think is wicked. There is no such thing as a Christian child. There is only a child of Christian parents. Why is our entire society happy to slap a label like Catholic or Protestant, Muslim or Jew, on a tiny child? Isn't that, when you think about it, a kind of mental child abuse?

Hermeneutic Question   Why does Dawkins believe it is wicked to raise children religiously?

The focus of this question isn't philosophical as such, but actually hermeneutic. Hermeneutic questions are often good places to start because they ensure understanding precedes analysis, and they allow the pupils' critical sense of the stimulus to emerge through a digestive rather than a vivisectionist process. A critical take on the stimulus will naturally emerge when giving interpretation; allow this to happen and then, when the discussion starts to take shape, set the following Task Question and allow a new talk time.

Task Question 2   Is raising children into a religion a form of abuse?

Questions to take you further

* Is there such a thing as a Muslim or Christian child?

* Is it wrong for adults to teach children their beliefs? Is this indoctrination?

* Are children capable of understanding religion?

* Are children responsible for their beliefs or are they hopelessly gullible?

* Should parents be left to raise their children as they wish? Is there a correct way to raise children?

* Is it unfair that we aren't able to choose the family we are born into?

* Are we defined by our families?

❖ Should children be free?

Display these statements on the board:

1.   'I don't believe in God.'

2.   'I have no beliefs about God.'

3.   'I believe that God doesn't exist.'

4.   'I don't live as though God exists.'

Task Question 3   Do these statements mean different things?

Questions to take you further

❖ Which of these statements are atheistic?

❖ Are theism, atheism and agnosticism our only options?

❖ If you are not for God, does that mean you are against Him?

❖ Do we all have beliefs about God? Is it possible to have no beliefs about God?

❖ If you say, 'God doesn't exist,' what does 'God' refer to in this statement?

❖ What is atheism?

On the board:

'I believe in God, but I don't show it in anything I do.'

Task Question 4   Does this statement make sense?

Questions to take you further

❖ How does one show that one believes in God? Simply by saying it?

❖ How does one show that one doesn't believe in God? Simply by saying it?

- ❖ Does a person's behaviour show us whether or not they believe in God?

- ❖ Could someone you know well believe in God without you realising it?

- ❖ Is it possible to hide your beliefs?

- ❖ Is it possible to live without religious beliefs?

- ❖ Is it possible to live without any beliefs whatsoever?

- ❖ What is belief?

The Problem of Evil

World is suddener than we fancy it.

Louis MacNeice

Starter Question 1   Should there be no suffering in the world?

Questions to take you further

- ❖ Is suffering a sign of a flawed world?

- ❖ Is there too much suffering in the world?

- ❖ What is suffering?

In the Gospel of Mark we learn of Jesus' suffering. He was arrested and put on trial before the high priest. Criminal charges were brought against him but he remained silent, neither conceding nor denying their truth. The high priest asked him, 'Why do you not speak?' Jesus did not reply. 'Are you the son of God?' the high priest asked. 'I am,' said Jesus, and he was sentenced to death.

A crown of thorns was placed on his head. He was mocked and beaten. They dressed him like a king and spat on him. Then, nailed to a cross, he was left to die.

After nine hours Jesus broke down beneath the darkened sky. With a desperate voice he cried,

Eloi, Eloi, lama sabachthani?

The language was Aramaic. It meant, 'My God, my God, why have you forsaken me?' He could not bear the pain, but God had done nothing to ease it. Sentenced to death for claiming to be God's son, Jesus now believed that God, his Father, had stopped caring.

Task Question 1   Does suffering show that God (if He exists) does not care about His creations?

Questions to take you further

❖ Can you love someone and let them suffer?

❖ All people suffer. Does that mean we are all victims?

❖ Is there always someone to blame for suffering?

❖ Are we so vulnerable that we need a god to care for us?

❖ What is care?

For thousands of years theists have tried to defend their belief in God against the claim that the existence of suffering proves that He does not exist.

Starter Question 2   How might suffering prove that there is no God?

This question encourages the pupils to make their own leap from the premise of suffering to the conclusion of God's non-existence. If they do make it, then present the argument below as a formalisation of their ideas, explaining that

this can help to make arguments clearer. If they don't, then take them through the argument, presenting the premises one at a time, discussing them as you go. At this stage, don't evaluate the premises, or the connections between them, just ensure that they are understood.

Before presenting the argument, make sure the class are comfortable with this format (see Appendix 6) and with the metamorphosis of the board discussed in the Introduction. You do not want the class to think that they are being taught the conclusion.

1.   If God is all powerful, He could stop suffering.
2.   If God is all loving, He would want to stop suffering.
3.   But there is suffering.
4.   So either God is weak, evil or He doesn't exist.
5.   But it doesn't make sense for God to be weak or evil.
6.   Therefore God doesn't exist.

You could present this variation on the final premise and conclusion if you wish to focus on God's attributes rather than His existence:

5.   But it doesn't make sense for God not to exist.
6.   Therefore God is either weak or evil.

Task Question 2   Is this a good argument?

Questions to take you further

❖   Does God have to be all powerful?
❖   Does God have to be all loving?
❖   Can suffering be good for us? Is pain ever good?
❖   If we didn't suffer, would we need God?

* Can you still believe in God even if the argument is good? Could you say, 'Yes, the argument is true, but I don't believe it'?

* Is the problem of evil a logical or an emotional problem?

Ask the class to identify which premises they would reject. In the unfortunate event of a consensus on the argument's strength, ask the class to consider how a theist might respond.

Many early Christians found it impossible to believe in Christ's embodiment, to imagine the son of God sweating and sneezing. Some argued that since the physical world of matter is impure Jesus could not have belonged to it; he didn't really have a material body, he only appeared to, it was an illusion (this view is called Docetism).

A hundred or so years after Jesus' death, Valentinus, a Gnostic theologian, addressed these concerns about the nature of God's incarnation in Christ. Valentinus said that though Jesus drank and ate, he did not go to the toilet. Divinity and shit were thought to be incompatible, which raises the question: is it conceivable for a pure and perfect God to have made a world constituted by the skin on cold gravy, lumpy milk, dried vomit, gangrene and maggots? How could a perfect God create a world that contains disgusting things? Why would He?

Perhaps disgust, just as much as suffering, proves that either God is imperfect, or He doesn't exist.

Task Question 3 Does disgust prove that there is no God?

Questions to take you further

* Would a perfect world contain disgusting things?

* Is the world ugly?

- Is disgust a response to what is bad about the world? Are children wrong to take pleasure in disgust?

- Is the problem with our attitude towards the world or with the world itself?

- Is evil disgusting? If so, how are torture and slavery like lumpy milk?

- Is disgust a moral reaction?

- If God made disgusting things, does that make God disgusting?

- What is disgust?

The Nature of Evil

Once we have taken Evil into ourselves, it no longer insists that we believe in it.

Franz Kafka

Starter Question 1   What evil acts and events have occurred in history?

By asking what makes those events evil, work towards building a mind-map for the following question:

Question to take you further

- What is evil?

As I've said, it's important with 'What is …' questions to try and find instances of 'What is not' – as Kent tells Lear, 'I'll teach you differences.' So if there's a consensus on evil, try to offer a few contentious examples, for example, the murder of Bin Laden, the British Empire, the bombing of Dresden, the Iraq War.

On 11 April 1961, the Israeli government put the Nazi war criminal Adolf Eichmann on trial in Jerusalem. During the war he had been in charge of transporting Jews to the death camps. It is estimated that over 3 million Jews were murdered in these camps.

In attendance was a writer named Hannah Arendt who had been sent by *The New Yorker* magazine to cover the trial. What she saw profoundly changed her understanding of evil. Formerly she had believed that the Nazis were radically evil, that a demonic motive lay at the root of their atrocities. But in Jerusalem Arendt was struck by the apparent lack of a dark drive in Eichmann. His concerns were seemingly ordinary and dull. He was interested in being awarded job promotions; he wanted to prove that he was an excellent employee, an efficient and dedicated worker. There seemed to be in him no mad passion for violence and death. How, then, could Eichmann do such evil? Arendt said that he was simply thoughtless, he was shallow. She called it banality.

At the trial Eichmann defended himself by claiming that he was only following orders. This, Arendt thought, was an example of how ordinary people can do evil things. Initially Eichmann was repulsed at the idea and prospect of the systematic genocide of the Jews, the so-called Final Solution. But over the course of a month he adapted and he changed his mind. He somehow overcame his disgust. How did this happen? Arendt claims that he just stopped thinking. He gave up his mind.

Eichmann's trial lasted 14 weeks and he was ultimately sentenced to death. He seemed unconcerned. He faced the gallows calmly, waving away the black hood customarily placed over the prisoner's head. 'Long live Germany,' he said, speaking his final words.

Task Question 1 *'How could someone be so evil?'*
'He was just very thoughtless.'
Is thoughtlessness a good explanation of evil?

Questions to take you further

* Is it possible to stop thinking?

* Is it possible to forget your feelings? Is it possible to do things you hate?

* Does thinking make us better people? Can it stop evil?

* Does evil come from the lack of something or the possession of something?

* Is evil a darkness of the soul?

* Is evil an illness?

* Should Eichmann have been executed?

* What is thinking?

Some pupils might resist the word 'evil' and it would be good to look into the reality and usefulness of the word, but, before doing so, you can still explore the Task Question without it: 'The question of whether there is such a thing as evil is an interesting one, which we'll return to. Would you agree that people tend to label horrific things as "evil"? And what do you think makes people do these horrific things? Is it thoughtlessness?'

Task Question 2   Can ordinary people do evil things?

Questions to take you further

* Is it just a matter of circumstance?

* Is it possible to immunise ourselves against our circumstances?

* Can we know what we are capable of?

* Is evil ordinary?

- ❖ Is evil a common part of our everyday life or is it something rare and anomalous?
- ❖ What is an ordinary person?
- ❖ Is there anyone that could never do evil?
- ❖ Can evil be eradicated?
- ❖ Is evil real?

Scepticism

Life's nonsense pierces us with strange relation.

Wallace Stevens

It's 1939. A short timid sort of man stands before a long hall of waiting faces. He shuffles his papers while the audience sigh and smoke. The room grows foggy. The man pats his pockets and clears his throat. The audience lean in, their red eyes squinting through the thinning air. Only the ticking of the clock can be heard.

The man, silhouetted by the light, slowly lifts his hands high above his head. Looking up at his right hand he says, 'Here is one hand.' He pauses. He looks at his left hand. 'And here is another.' He stops, looks into the distance, and falls silent, his hands still held high.

The hall becomes an aviary of twitching eyelids… A few bated seconds pass… Then all at once the audience bursts like a bladder.

Whole rows start wailing with laughter, holding their stomachs, rocking in their chairs. Some applaud and applaud even louder when they realise they are using their hands to do so. Some turn to their neighbours and say, 'What good common sense he has,' and they all nod together in agreement. Others scoff and scowl: 'What utter *nonsense*.

Has he lost his mind?' Someone somewhere is screaming, 'You're wrong! *Wrong!*' A few sit in studied contemplation. An old gent in the corner dribbles in his sleep.

Hermeneutic Question   What do you think is going on in the story?

Questions to take you further

- Why did the man hold up his hands and tell us what they are?

- Why did the audience react in that way?

- Who might the man be?

- Where might he be?

- What might be the purpose of the event?

The hand-man is a philosopher called G. E. Moore. His audience are also philosophers. The story is a dramatisation of an essay he wrote, in which he responds to the 'problem' of scepticism; the problem, that is, of whether we can know anything at all, of whether we can even know that the world exists. Moore's essay suggests that doubting the existence of the world is as absurd as doubting the existence of one's hands, which is very absurd indeed.

Three hundred years before Moore's essay, René Descartes, the so-called Father of Modern Philosophy, had decided to test the quality of his knowledge by seeing whether it could withstand radical doubt, which is analogous to blowing up a building to see how strong it is. He wanted to discover what, if anything, he could know for certain. Such an endeavour, he warned, should only be undertaken once in a lifetime.

Descartes' project led him to believe that the only thing he could know for certain was that his mind exists. Everything else was questionable.

Dreams trick us into thinking they are real, so perhaps everything we believe to be real is actually a vast inescapable dream. Or perhaps our experiences are a masterful illusion created by a malign power manipulating our malleable minds. Can we know that we are not being toyed with, that the entire world isn't an elaborate hoax? Is this idea beyond doubt?

Descartes suggested that – unless we believe in God it is not beyond doubt. The existence of the world can be questioned and therefore cannot be known. The only thing that can be known is that our own particular thinking mind exists. Only this is guaranteed (we cannot doubt that we are thinking because doubting is thinking). Everything else is uncertain, unknown.

Moore's essay attempts to bypass this scepticism. He believes he can prove that there is a world because it is beyond doubt that he has hands, which are part of the world. Descartes is denying something so obvious it is silly. By showing us his hands, Moore was saying, 'Look! The world exists! I know it does. Because my hands exist. I know they do. Because here they are.'

'What good common sense he has.'

- ❖ Have you ever said you know that you have hands? Is it common sense you've ever used?

- ❖ Is there such a thing as useless common sense?

'What utter *nonsense*. Has he lost his mind?'

- ❖ Does Moore sound mad?

- ❖ Do people ever say, 'I know I have hands'? Is it a meaningful remark?

- ❖ Can scepticism be disproved?

'You're wrong! *Wrong!*'

* Does Moore know that he has hands?
* Is it beyond doubt that Moore has hands?

Task Question 1   Which of the above responses do you most agree with?

Questions to take you further

* Does the story's context change your view of the events?
* Does the story's context make it more/less understandable?
* What sounds sillier: 'I know I have hands,' or, 'I don't know anything at all'?

Task Question 2   Is it possible to doubt that the world exists?

Questions to take you further

* Is it madness to doubt that the world exists?
* Is it sensible to doubt that the world exists?
* Is it morally wrong to doubt that the world exists?
* Are many of our beliefs beyond doubt?
* If we can doubt something, does that mean we don't know it?
* Do we know that the world exists?
* Do we *need* to know that the world exists? Would it matter if we didn't know?
* Is it dangerous to doubt that the world exists?
* Is the existence of the world known, unknown or unknowable?
* Is it possible that the world doesn't exist?

Logic

We must live in this confusion as if it were the salt of existence.

Richard Poirier

You may wish to start by presenting this conversation to the class (a photocopiable version of this is available in Appendix 1).

A father said to his son, 'Son, listen to me, I have something very important to tell you: you must never trust anyone or anything.'

'Why?' the boy asked.

'Because people are usually lying or mistaken. The opposite of what they say is more likely to be true,' said the father.

'What about you? Should I trust you?'

'No, you can't even trust me.'

'So is the opposite of what you say more likely to be true?' questioned the boy.

'Yes, that's right.'

'But you said I shouldn't trust anyone. Does that mean I should actually trust everyone?'

'Yes, that's right,' nodded the father.

'And since you say that's right, does that mean it may be wrong?'

'Indeed.'

'Which means I shouldn't actually trust anyone?'

'Certainly! You must never trust anyone.'

'And can I trust you when you tell me this?' the boy asked.

'No, no – you mustn't,' said the father.

'And since you say I mustn't, does that mean I must?'

'You've understood me perfectly, my boy.'

Starter Question 1   Is this good advice?

Questions to take you further

- Is it always bad advice to tell someone to both do something and not do it?
- Is confusing advice ever good advice?
- Is advice better the simpler it is?
- What things are made better by being simpler?
- What things are made worse by being simpler?
- Is it possible to understand the father perfectly?

There are two dialogues to this session. They'd be better acted than read (a photocopiable version of this is available in Appendix 2).

A woman is on trial for the alleged murder of her husband.

Barrister Where were you the night of your husband's murder?

Defendant I was staying at my sister's in Bristol.

Barrister Had you spent the day there?

Defendant No, I arrived late afternoon.

Barrister From your home in Cuddesdon?

Defendant Yes.

Barrister At approximately what time?

Defendant About 4.30.

Barrister How long is it in the car from Cuddesdon to Bristol? About an hour and a half?

Defendant About that.

Barrister So you must have left your house at about 3?

Defendant Yes.

Barrister And you are a doctor, is that right?

Defendant Yes.

Barrister So this was a Sunday. Did you not have work the next day in Oxford?

Defendant Yes, I did.

Barrister Why then were you staying at your sister's all the way in Bristol? That's rather a long commute.

Defendant My husband and I had had an argument. I didn't want to be there.

Barrister The last time you saw your husband alive was after an argument?

Defendant Yes.

Barrister Were you angry?

Defendant Yes.

Barrister And then you drove to your sister's in Bristol?

Defendant Yes.

Barrister It was snowing that day, wasn't it?

Defendant Yes.

Barrister What's it like to drive through Cuddesdon in the snow?

Defendant Not easy.

Barrister How much snow fell that day?

Defendant Maybe two feet.

Barrister Those conditions must have been almost impossible.

Defendant Yes.

Barrister So you're feeling emotional, there's two feet of snow – how did you manage to get to your sister's in the ordinary hour and a half?

Defendant I left before it got heavy.

Barrister Did you not just say that there was two feet of snow?

Defendant Yes, but I didn't mean in Cuddesdon. That was how much there was at my sister's.

Barrister Right, and you arrived there at about 4.30.

Defendant Yes, well I think so. Maybe it was closer to 5.30.

Barrister It must have been getting very dark by then.

Defendant Yes.

Barrister Is it true that the week before your husband's murder you received a ticket because your headlights weren't working?

Defendant … yes, that's correct.

Barrister Had they been repaired by the time of your journey to Bristol?

Defendant … no.

Barrister Am I right in thinking, then, that you drove to your sister's house in a state of emotional distress, through the snow and in the dark, without the use of your headlights?

Defendant I must have left earlier than that, before it got dark. It was probably closer to 2.

Barrister Did you not just tell the court that you left at 3?

Defendant Yes.

Barrister You left at 2 and you also left at 3. So it would follow then that at 2.30 you were both in Cuddesdon and not in Cuddesdon at the same time. Is that right?

Defendant I'm not sure.

Hermeneutic Question 1   Do you trust this testimony?

If the class's discussion does not naturally converge on this moment, focus on the last line from the barrister; ask if there is a problem with the inference made. Try to draw out the law of non-contradiction – a statement p and its negation not-p cannot both be true, i.e. there are no true contradictions – from the pupils' responses. Inform the class that this is widely regarded as a logical 'law', a pre-condition of reason, but that for the time being you will be regarding it as a hypothesis. Aristotle believed that contradictions were not only false but inconceivable. As an experiment you could test Aristotle's claim by asking the class whether they can imagine the barrister's inference being true.

The second dialogue involves the same situation, but imagines the line of questioning taking a different turn.

Barrister Where were you the night of your husband's murder?

Defendant I was staying at my sister's in Bristol.

Barrister Had you spent the day there?

Defendant No, I arrived late afternoon.

Barrister From your home in Cuddesdon?

Defendant Yes.

Barrister Why were you staying with her?

Defendant My husband and I had had a fight.

Barrister What about?

Defendant For the past few months he had been talking about moving, living abroad. I didn't want to.

Barrister What sort of man was your husband?

Defendant He was difficult.

Barrister In what way was he difficult?

Defendant He was stubborn, proud; ashamed.

Barrister What was he ashamed of?

Defendant I don't know.

Barrister Was your husband an alcoholic?

Defendant No, but he drank.

Barrister Did he drink too much?

Defendant Yes.

Barrister What do you mean by too much?

Defendant He would just get argumentative. He had a short temper. He wouldn't stop once he got started.

Barrister What would he argue about?

Defendant He blamed me for lots of things. For not being as successful as I could be, for not appreciating him.

Barrister Did you love your husband?

Defendant Yes.

Barrister You loved your husband despite the drinking and the anger and the attacks on your character.

Defendant …

Barrister Were he and your sister on good terms?

Defendant No.

Barrister Why not?

Defendant She never really trusted him.

Barrister Was there a money issue between them?

Defendant … yes.

Barrister What happened?

Defendant She owned a business, a small film production company. The company wasn't doing well. She needed to borrow some money. I didn't have enough and my husband refused to help.

Barrister What happened to the company?

Defendant It was liquidated.

Barrister How did you feel towards your husband for letting that happen?

Defendant I hated him for it.

Barrister You hated your husband?

Defendant Yes.

Barrister Did you ever hate him when he drank and argued?

Defendant I always hated him.

Barrister You always hated your husband?

Defendant Yes.

Barrister But did you not just tell the court that you loved him?

Defendant Yes.

Barrister Let's be clear on this. Did you love your husband or did you hate him?

Defendant Both. Both those things.

Barrister You both loved and hated your husband at the same time?

Defendant Yes.

Hermeneutic Question 2 Do you trust this testimony?

Questions to take you further

❖ Is the conjunction of love and hate a contradiction?

❖ Is hate the negation of love? Is love the negation of hate?

❖ If so, is the defendant lying or is the law of non-contradiction wrong?

- ❖ Can you hate something you love and love something you hate?
- ❖ Why might this testimony be trustworthy where the previous one is not?
- ❖ Do feeling and believing have different logical laws?
- ❖ Can feeling be separated from belief?

Again, if the class's discussion does not naturally converge on this moment, hold up for consideration the last line from the barrister. Consider whether it is independently plausible, whether it is logically similar to the line from the previous dialogue and whether it undermines the hypothesised law of non-contradiction.

Task Question 1   Can something be both true and false at the same time?

Questions to take you further

- ❖ Is the world ordered? Is it well-organised? Does it make sense?
- ❖ Can the world be neatly divided into truth and falsity?
- ❖ Is the difference between truth and falsity absolute or is it vague?
- ❖ Can an emotion and its negation both be present simultaneously?
- ❖ Is it possible to believe a contradiction?

These Task Questions may seem repetitive insofar as it was implicit in the previous Hermeneutic Questions. The point of the Task Question is to use the thoughts already raised to reach a general idea about the logical status of contradictions, to shift the focus from the narrow to the broad. But also, repetition is rarely a concern in philosophy. You could run the same session with the same class several times and it will always be different. This is partly thanks to the aeolian motion of the mind, and also to the oral nature of the sessions. Thoughts can become hopelessly consecrated when written down.

These are further questions you might hold up for consideration:

❖ Can a thing be what it is not?

❖ Can a thing both exist and not exist?

❖ Is it possible to believe something you don't believe?

❖ Can a team both win and lose a match?

❖ Can a person be both full-up and starving?

It can be fun to throw in the liar paradox when discussing contradictions. Write on the board, 'This sentence is false,' then ask the class whether the sentence is true or not. Since the sentence says it is false, it seems that if it were false, then it would be true, but if it were true, then it would be false. Pupils sometimes conclude that the sentence is both true and false. Sometimes they conclude it is neither because it is meaningless.

Imagine that a politician, campaigning to become the next prime minister, was asked to give an outline of her personal feelings towards life, and this is what she said:

I believe in God but I think we are alone.

I am scared of nothing but I am always hiding.

I believe in war but I am against violence.

I want to please others but I want to be free.

I want to be safe but I want to take risks.

I am a kind person but I don't care about others.

I am good to my friends but I often lie to them.

I believe in sharing but I think people are out to exploit you.

I like being rich but I don't like always getting what I want.

I want everything to stay the same but I want it all to change.

I think humans are mere animals but I think we have a soul.

I know an awful lot but I hardly know a thing.
I believe everyone is equal but I think I am better than most.
I think family is good but I think family is hell.

Task Question 2   Does her statement make her an unappealing candidate?

Questions to take you further

* Would you prefer consistent or inconsistent politicians? *(Machiavelli leaders)*

* Is it bad to be inconsistent?

* Is consistency desirable?

* Is absolute consistency possible?

* Are our minds unified whole things?

* Is consistency compatible with change?

* Does inconsistency undermine the possibility of, or the need for, trust?

* Is it worse to be inconsistent in our beliefs rather than our emotions?

* If our minds reflected the way of the world, would they be consistent or inconsistent?

* Is the soliloquy inconsistent?

Human Omniscience

The beginning of paranoia is the deep sense that it all hangs together.

David Trotter

Starter Question   What is science?

Questions to take you further

❖ Is it a method?

❖ Is it a myth?

❖ Is it a perspective on the world?

❖ Is it an authority?

❖ Is it an institution?

❖ Is it a religion?

❖ Is it the truth?

❖ What is it for?

Lord Kelvin was a Scottish scientist who thought it all made sense. From the 16th to the 20th century massive advances had taken place in physics: Copernicus had proposed that the sun and not the Earth is at the centre of the solar system; Kepler had arrived at laws which describe the motion of planets; Newton had developed laws of motion and universal gravity, realising that the same forces which govern falling apples and tennis balls also govern the stars and planets; it had been seen that light behaves like a wave; and Maxwell had established the relationship between electricity and magnetism.

With these advances behind him, Lord Kelvin reputedly stood before an audience at the turn of the 20th century and told them the news. 'There is nothing new to be discovered in physics now,' he said.

Yet just a few decades later physics had been revolu-
tionised. Kelvin's announcement had preceded the
discoveries that the universe is expanding and that
the Milky Way is just one galaxy among many; it
was before the Big Bang theory, before Einstein
overturned Newton's conception of space and time,
before it was understood that light behaves like a particle as well
as a wave, before E = mc². It came before the shock of discovering the
strange and unpredictable behaviour of the sub-atomic world.

Lord Kelvin had spoken too soon.

Task Question 1 Will science ever end?

Questions to take you further

❖ Will science end because there are limits to human
understanding?

❖ Will science end because there are no limits to human
understanding?

❖ Does science progress?

❖ Does science give us knowledge or only probable belief?

❖ Will technology continue to progress forever?

❖ Will medicine ever end?

❖ Does science explain the world or interpret it?

❖ Is the universe infinitely complicated?

Physics strives for simplicity and elegance. Newton's
laws of gravitation had elegantly shown that the same
force, gravity, which affects the behaviour of objects in
our everyday experience, also affects the behaviour
of massive objects such as stars and planets.
Newton had managed to unify our understanding

of the everyday with our understanding of the heavens. A single force governs many things.

James Clerk Maxwell had accomplished a similar feat when he uncovered the connections between electricity and magnetism. He combined these to describe a single force: electromagnetism. Physics had achieved further unification.

Physicists now believe that there are four forces which govern all things within the universe: gravity, electromagnetism, the strong nuclear force (which binds the nucleus of an atom together) and the weak nuclear force (which is the force behind radiation). In the pursuit of elegance physicists are attempting to unify these four forces into a single theory. They have succeeded in doing so with all forces except one: gravity.

Quantum mechanics describes the behaviour of matter on a microscopic level (the level of electromagnetism and the weak and strong nuclear forces). But according to quantum mechanics the universe behaves in peculiar ways; the microscopic world is random and vague.

In the world of large objects we can calculate the behaviour of bodies with certainty. For example, if we were to fire a cannon, we could work out exactly where the cannonball would land. But in the world of the very small, we can only calculate the behaviour of things like electrons with probability. When it comes down to the tiny, the universe is a game of dice.

Our theory of gravity – called general relativity – isn't at all like this. Gravity describes the world of large objects, like cannonballs and stars. Whereas quantum mechanics sees the world as flickering and frantic, general relativity describes the world as smooth and curvaceous. The universe of tiny things and the universe of large things seem perplexingly different, as though they were of different worlds, yet they describe the same world.

Physicists want a theory of everything: one theory that will unify all of nature's laws. They have sought to unify general relativity with quantum mechanics, but so far they have been unable to piece them together. It's like asking Ornette Coleman to jam with Mozart.

Some physicists are unhappy with the present situation. They believe that the universe must be coherent, that all the forces of nature must work in harmony. There must be a single set of laws that can describe everything. The universe cannot be both graceful (as general relativity suggests) and cacophonous (as quantum mechanics suggests). It must all hang together. It must make sense.

Task Question 2   Should the universe make sense?

Questions to take you further

❖ Does it make sense to say that it makes sense that the universe doesn't make sense?

❖ What is wrong with nonsense?

❖ Is elegance a virtue?

❖ Is it possible to see everything at once?

❖ Is the universe a single thing?

❖ Will we find a theory of everything?

Because the above overview is rather abstract, it would be helpful to complement the descriptions with pictures. Searching Google for 'general relativity' will provide plenty of images of objects warping spacetime, illustrating the euphonious geometry of the theory. The point is only to convey the gist of the incompatibility between macroscopic and microscopic, so perhaps music would also help, with, say, the first movement of Mozart's Symphony No. 25 representing general relativity, and John Cage's Music of Changes representing quantum mechanics.

It has been argued by the scientist Roger Penrose that a theory of everything will not cut the mustard unless it can explain consciousness. An all-encompassing theory of the world should reveal how an assembly of atoms, such as a human brain, can give rise to experience. It should tell us how it is possible for feelings and sensations to arise out of a mass of unfeeling matter.

Some philosophers, however, believe that we will never understand consciousness, that consciousness is a stretch too far for any theory. We are animals adapted to survive. Our intelligence evolved simply to ensure our survival, to solve problems of the immediate environment, to cook soup and make penicillin. Our minds and their capacities are shaped for life on Earth; they are not capable of understanding the nature of reality or unlocking the mysteries of consciousness. We are featherless bipeds with canine teeth and opposable thumbs. Just as ants will never compose symphonies, we will never possess a complete understanding of the world. It's simply beyond us.

Task Question 3   Do humans lack the intelligence to fully understand the world?

Questions to take you further

*   Would we need to step outside of ourselves to understand reality? Can we do this?

*   Could any natural living creature fully understand the world?

*   Is our intelligence simply a tool to live?

*   Would it be good to know everything?

*   Is there such a thing as reality in itself?

*   Would our lives be any different if we did fully understand the world?

*   Do we understand the world better than ants do?

*   Why don't ants write symphonies?

Facts and Opinions

I only know what I believe.

Tony Blair

I wrote this session for a class who believed that truth lay exclusively with the hard sciences while anything debatable was a matter of opinion. The session is partly one about the scope of philosophy, but it also addresses questions on the borders between the private and the public, the limits of tolerance, the bounds of conflict and the value of argument.

Hermeneutic Question 'Everyone has the right to their own opinion.' What does this mean?

Starter Question 1 Do we have the right to our own facts?

Use their answers to establish definitions for 'fact' and 'opinion'. Ask how facts are proved and whether they can always be proved. Ask whether it makes sense to speak of proving opinions.

a. 'I know that murder is wrong.'

b. 'I believe that murder is wrong.'

c. 'It is my opinion that murder is wrong.'

Starter Question 2 Which of the above statements would you use?

Use their reasons to uncover the implications of these different words: 'know', 'believe' and 'opinion'. Ideas considered might be that 'know' implies truth and is therefore objective, that 'belief' can betray doubt about an objective matter, and that 'opinion' indicates a subjective viewpoint. It may also be said that 'opinion' is a consequence of humility or tolerance or cowardice, that 'know' expresses conviction or hubris or justification, and that 'belief' conveys faith or doubt or private passion.

For the following Task Questions divide the board into two columns: one for 'Matters of Fact' and the other for 'Matters of Opinion'. It is sometimes necessary to emphasise that falsehoods belong in the 'Matters of Fact' column.

1. 'Water is H_2O.'

2. 'Cauliflower is vile.'

3. 'The Prime Minister is ruining the country.'

4. 'It is my opinion that the Prime Minister is ruining the country.'

5. 'Einstein was a genius.'

Task Question 1   In which columns do the above statements belong?

1. 'The universe started with the Big Bang.'

2. 'The sun will rise tomorrow.'

3. 'The glass is half empty.'

4. 'Hitler was good for the world.'

5. 'Only I exist.'

Task Question 2   In which columns do the above statements belong?

1. 'It is wrong to humiliate others.'

2. 'To be rich is an excellent goal in life.'

3. 'No matter your colour, gender, nationality or sexual orientation, all people are equal.'

4. 'My grandmother was a truly great woman.'

5. 'God exists.'

Task Question 3 In which columns do the above statements belong?

Allow for, or even suggest, the possibility of there being a third (or more) column. Pupils may find that the dualism of facts and opinions is not enough to encompass the variety of statements.

Objects and Essences

You know how you know when someone's telling lies? you said. They get their story right every time, down to the last word.

Ciaran Carson

Walking in the shadow of skyscrapers you find a door. Behind the door a passageway unwinds in a line of beauty through to a window overlooking a room. You climb through the window and drop into the room. The room is odd. The most noticeable thing about it is that it contains no objects, none at all.

Starter Question What is in the room?

Questions to take you further

❖ Is air in the room?

❖ Is heat in the room?

❖ Is light in the room?

❖ Is time in the room?

❖ Is space in the room?

Task Question 1   What is an object?

You can approach this question by taking a provisional definition from a pupil and opening it up to the class, asking if they can think of any counterexamples (which will be an object that the definition doesn't include or a non-object that it does). Once a counterexample is raised, ask how the provisional definition could be modified to accommodate it. Then, once again, see if there are any counterexamples to the modified definition, and so on.

Below is a stock of possible counterexamples.

+ Is air an object?

+ Is the past an object?

+ Are dreams objects?

+ Is fear an object?

+ Is fire an object?

+ Is the universe an object?

+ Is life an object?

+ Are words objects?

+ Are days objects?

+ Is light an object? Is dark an object?

+ Is music an object?

+ Is the taste of vanilla an object?

+ Is the smell of coffee an object?

+ Is emptiness an object?

+ Is God an object?

Besides the fun of toying with the metaphysics of these various 'objects' (a charming discussion once followed from a pupil's suggestion that an object is something you can break; we wondered why you can't break water), the discus-

sion should also serve to expose the nebulous meaning of the word 'object', which is a prelude to …

Task Question 2 Is there any word that has a clear and definite meaning?

Questions to take you further

❖ Are most words vague?

❖ Can the world be divided into definite and distinct entities? (You might address this question by asking the class to empty their pockets and count how many things they have in them – is the answer simple or contentious?)

❖ Is the world vague?

❖ Is perfect communication possible?

❖ Do dictionaries prove that language does have clear and definite meanings? (You might address this question by choosing an arbitrary dictionary definition and asking the class whether they think it offers a complete and thorough account of the word.)

❖ We need words to define words. Is there anything philosophically significant about this?

In the early 20th century, philosophers began to feel that their philosophical confusions were a sort of joke, that something, or someone, was fooling them, leading them down dead ends and round in circles. They wondered why, after so many thousands of years of doing philosophy, they always ended up back where they started. Why hadn't they made any real progress and actually solved some problems? They believed that their endless perplexity wasn't a function of the difficulty of the questions they faced but of the tenacity of the trap they were in. They were being toyed with, and the culprit was language.

Language was the primary source of their philosophical confusions. Because so many of our words lack clear and definite boundaries, when we try to understand or use them precisely we find ourselves waylaid by a fog of meaning. Language looks deceptively ordered, yet it entangles and ensnares us. Philosophy searches for clarity, its medium is language, yet trying to attain clarity in language is like trying to scale a waterfall or lasso a cloud.

This view of language led philosophers to believe that many of the problems they had been trying to solve – What is the mind? Can we know there is a world? Is beauty real? – were fake linguistic mirages; they called them 'pseudo-problems'. Philosophers, such as the logical positivists, tried to police language to avoid these pseudo-problems. They tried to ensure that we were as precise as possible in our use of words. Statements which had no clear and definite meaning were called 'pseudo-statements'.

Some philosophers went beyond merely policing language. They proposed that the best way to avoid confusion and bewitchment would be to invent a new ideal language. Bertrand Russell, for example, believed that common language was not sufficiently logical – he even feared mathematics was not sufficiently logical – and in order to avoid error and confusion we would need to construct a logically perfect language. Such a language would be neither vague nor ambiguous, its words – or 'symbols' – would have clear and definite meanings. Without this crystalline language, our attempts to properly understand the world would be forever thwarted by indeterminacy and nonsense.

Task Question 3   Could we invent a perfectly precise language?

Questions to take you further

❖   Do we need a more precise language?

- Are vagueness and ambiguity a problem?
- Are vagueness and ambiguity inescapable?
- Does language affect our understanding of the world?
- Can language be invented? Who invented English?
- Russell wrote, 'The essential business of language is to assert or deny facts.' Is it?
- What is the essential business of language?
- Does the need for metaphor show that language is descriptively inadequate?

Erasure

Our faithlessness to our language repeats our faithlessness to all our shared commitments.

Stanley Cavell

Imagine a secret book stored in the cavernous underbelly of the British Library. It is the most powerful book in the world and for that reason there is no one in the world able to access it.

Years ago the government considered using it for what they believed to be the greater public good, but they prudently decided that the effects of doing so were too unpredictable: they could not calculate the potential consequences of their potential actions. Since destroying the book was not an option, the government arranged for it to be locked away in perpetuity. Enclosed in a safe that set its own code, inaccessible to everyone, the book has been banished ever since.

The book is a dictionary that sits at the centre of the mystical nexus of language, connected to every book and all dictionaries, both physical and mental. Every entry is written in pencil. Rubbing one out has the effect of erasing the word from every book, every dictionary and everyone – the word is deleted from humanity's collective memory, which explains why destroying the entire book was not an option.

When the book was last read gaps could be seen, the faint trace of lead, the frayed snow of rubber, a conspicuous emptiness. It had been used before. What the missing words were, of course, we'll never know.

Imagine you held this book in your possession. You fancy erasing the word 'true'. *Poof.*

Starter Question 1   What other words would disappear with it?

Questions to take you further

- ❖ How many other words only make sense in relation to the word 'true'?
- ❖ Does every word connect to every other?

Task Question 1   Would the world be better without this word and its companions?

Questions to take you further

- ❖ Would the world change without it?
- ❖ Do words influence the way we think?
- ❖ Do words influence the way we act?
- ❖ What *can't* words do? Is there a limit to their power?

❖ Could 'true' be expressed through other words?

After decimating truth you continue flicking through the book. Your eye falls on 'love'. *Poof.*

Starter Question 2   What other words would disappear with it?

Question to take you further

❖ How many other words only make sense in relation to the word 'love'?

Task Question 2   Would the world be better without this word and its companions?

Questions to take you further

❖ Can we be enslaved by words? Can we become trapped in them?

❖ Does language describe our experience or shape it?

❖ Could 'love' be expressed through other words?

❖ Would people still fall in love even if they had never heard of it?

Starter Question 3   What words would you erase from the book? What words would disappear with it?

Question to take you further

❖ Are there any words you could erase that would wipe out all others?

Task Question 3   Would the world be better without this word and its companions?

With the final questions you could take a whole range of responses from the class and discuss these in turn. As an additional activity, you might also want to think of examples of things we lack words for, of the absences in our language, the possible victims of erasure. When we are struggling to find the right word, is this the result of a kind of erasure? Do you imagine the book to be more populated by existing words or erased ones? You could also refer to Wittgenstein's famous sentence, 'What we cannot speak about we must pass over in silence', and ask the class what they think this means and whether it has any connection to the session's story.

Finally, you might ask:

Task Question 4   What would happen if the whole book was burnt to ash?

Questions to take you further

❖ Would we be able to think?

❖ Would we know anything?

❖ Would we still have relationships?

❖ Would our experience of the world change?

Newness

Invention, it must be humbly admitted, does not consist in creating out of void, but out of chaos.

Mary Shelley

In the 1930s and 1940s, the painter Han van Meegeren became a multimillionaire through forging the works of the 17th century Dutch artist, Johannes Vermeer.

Van Meegeren had started out as an artist in his own right. His first show in 1917 was a success, receiving positive reviews, but his second show, five years later, garnered little praise. One critic concluded, 'A gifted technician who has made a sort of composite facsimile of the Renaissance school, he has every virtue except originality.'

Van Meegeren felt his work was being unjustly eclipsed by the ostentatious childishness of modern art. Looking back at this time he would later say, 'Driven into a state of anxiety and depression due to the all-too-meagre appreciation of my work, I decided, one fateful day, to revenge myself on the art critics and experts by doing something the likes of which the world had never seen before.' If he couldn't be appreciated for his own work, he would wear the mask of an Old Master and cheat his way to admiration.

With industry and care, van Meegeren began experimenting with ways of cosmetically aging pictures. He struck upon an effective process (using Bakelite and ovens) that enabled him to make new paintings appear three centuries old. Borrowing from Caravaggio's *Emmaus* picture, he then painted *The Supper at Emmaus*. Signed with Vermeer's monogram, this would become his greatest lie.

In 1937, van Meegeren passed the painting on to Abraham Bredius, a respected art historian, in the hope that it would be deemed authentic. Bredius not only judged it to be genuine, he hailed it as the greatest of all Vermeer's masterpieces. The picture was subsequently bought by the Boijmans Museum (where it still hangs) for the equivalent of $6 million and placed centre stage in the museum's exhibition, '400 Years of European Art'.

Though not everyone was convinced by these 'Vermeers', the truth only became public when van Meegeren himself confessed, indeed, when he was forced to confess in order to save his neck.

Unfortunately for van Meegeren, one of his forgeries had found its way into the possession of the Nazi minister, Hermann Göring. When the Second World War ended, officers from the Allied Art Commission, who were responsible for returning artworks that had been looted by the Nazis, traced the painting in Göring's collection back to van Meegeren, and he was arrested on suspicion of collaboration, of handing over a Dutch national treasure to the enemy.

Van Meegeren was caught between two crimes: fraud and treason. The former would issue a lesser punishment and so he confessed. To prove that Göring's painting was a fake, he was ordered by the court to paint his final Vermeer, which he did, demonstrating his (ambiguous) innocence and becoming a national hero: the man who fooled the Nazis.

In November 1947, he was sentenced to a year in prison, but died a month later, his body weakened by years of morphine and alcohol addiction.

Task Question 1   Which paintings are more valuable, the genuine or the forged?

With this question let's ignore the fact that van Meegeren's pictures are guff and don't actually look like Vermeer's. Let's pretend they're faultless imitations. It would be good to show the class a few real Vermeers alongside The Supper at Emmaus.

Questions to take you further

* Is an original more valuable than a copy?

* Is an art forger an artist?

* Do artists forge reality?

* Is the value of art purely in the way it looks or also in how it is made?

* Does how it is made change the way it looks? Does it change what we see when we look at it?

* Does an artist churning out pictures in their established style constitute self-forgery?

❖ Should Andy Warhol's *Brillo Boxes* – replications of a commercial shipping carton – count as forgeries? Are they original?

❖ If a forgery is a lie, what is the lie? How does it cheat our sense of reality?

Either individually or in groups, ask the class to make something that is original, new and unique. This exercise can be tied to English, music or drama. It might be an original drawing, sentence or sound. Present a few attempts and accompany each with the following question:

Starter Question 1   Is this completely original?

Question to take you further

❖ Are artists like God? Do they create their work just as God created the world?

Task Question 2   Is there such a thing as an original idea?

Questions to take you further

❖ Are thoughts creations of the mind?

❖ Are our minds creations? If so, who created them? If not, what are they?

❖ *Ex nihilo* is Latin for 'out of nothing'. Can anything be created *ex nihilo*?

❖ Would it be wrong for a tennis player to copy someone else's technique?

❖ Is plagiarism wrong?

At the beginning of his autobiography, the philosopher Jean-Jacques Rousseau wrote: 'I am made unlike anyone I have ever met; I will even venture to say that I am like no one in the whole world. I may be no better, but at least I am different.'

Hermeneutic Question   Could it be true that Rousseau was like no one in the world?

Questions to take you further

- ❖ Is everyone like someone else? Are we all versions of other people?

- ❖ Is everyone like everyone else? Is humanity a single person multiplied?

- ❖ Are some people more original than others?

- ❖ Are we creations? If so, who is our creator? If not, what are we?

- ❖ Is it good to be different? Is it bad to be the same?

Task Question 3   Is anything ever completely new?

Questions to take you further

- ❖ Is everything connected to and shaped by the past?

- ❖ Is everything a copy of something else?

- ❖ Is surprise a sign of something new?

- ❖ Is today completely new?

- ❖ Is anything ever exactly the same?

- ❖ What is newness?

Self

'*I*'

… an idea is 'true' so long as to believe it is profitable to our lives.
William James

Privacy

Human beings do not go hand in hand the whole stretch of the way.

Virginia Woolf

The word 'surveillance' comes from the French *sur* and *veiller*, meaning 'watch over'. Though the word only dates back to the 19th century, the idea of being watched over has been with us for a very long time. We are, for instance, told in a sura of the Qur'an that we cannot hide from God, and St Augustine similarly wrote, addressing God, that 'there is no place whatever where man may hide away from you' (as Adam and Eve discovered).

In the modern world God's surveillance was thought insufficient. The Anabaptists in 16th century Germany commanded that just as people cannot hide from God, nor should they hide from their fellows. In Münster, a town they ruled over, it was illegal to keep doors closed. Every house was ordered to leave its doors open. Privacy was forbidden.

Surveillance becomes somewhat harder when you are dealing with entire countries rather than individual towns. In the 20th century, the government of the Soviet Union wanted to keep a close and unblinking eye on all its 150 million citizens. But this was before the use of CCTV. The government overcame the lack of technology by turning each of its citizens into walking human cameras, spying on each other always.

It was illegal in the Soviet Union not to report any criminal behaviour you were in any way aware of. If you overheard your neighbour speaking of their hatred for the government, and you did not report this to the police, you could be imprisoned for up to ten years. If you did report it, however, you would be rewarded and regarded as a hero of the state.

The government would also employ ordinary people to spy for them. They employed doctors, priests, teenagers – anyone they thought was opportunely placed to watch over others. If you refused, you would be either imprisoned or deported to Siberia. By turning everyone into a spy the government became omnipresent. Surveillance was total.

Today Britain has a reputation as one of the most watched-over countries in the world. According to a 2013 report by the British Security Industry Association, the conservative estimate is 4 million CCTV cameras. On average we are watched by 300 cameras a day. Lying below ground, beneath Piccadilly Circus, there is a room laced with monitors that record every street in central London every second of the day.

Cameras are found in most schools and an increasing number of schools are installing CCTV in toilets and changing rooms.

Starter Question   Do we need surveillance?

Questions to take you further

* Should there be surveillance in our homes?

* Should our thoughts be under surveillance? Are there things we shouldn't think?

* Is privacy more valuable than safety?

* Do we need privacy? Are we all separate individuals?

* Is there such a thing as too much privacy?

* How much surveillance is too much surveillance?

* Why do we act differently when we know we are being watched?

❖ Do social media, such as Facebook, show that we do not want private lives?

❖ What is privacy?

The final bullet point can be approached by considering the contrast between the public and private. Are kidnappings and murders matters of public concern or are they private afflictions? Should they be reported in the news? Is a private space one in which the law doesn't apply? If the law is omnipresent, does that mean we never have total privacy? When we are in private, are we outside of society? Or are we always within society? Is privacy detachment? Does privacy place us beyond the remit of morality?

Part of the wish behind societies committed to mass surveillance is that by watching their citizens they will know them.

Imagine that, in Britain, rather than being watched by 300 cameras a day, you are watched by just one, but this one camera follows you everywhere you go. It watches and sees everything you do, from the day you were born to the present moment.

Task Question 1   Would someone watching the footage of this camera know you completely?

Questions to take you further

❖ Would they know you better than your friends and family do?

❖ What would they know about you? What wouldn't they know about you?

❖ Given their ability to replay your recorded past, their total knowledge of your history, would they know you better than you know yourself?

❖ Is it possible to live a life without secrets?

❖ Are there things – thoughts, feelings, beliefs – that we don't express through our actions?

* Are there things that we can hide in our actions? Is it possible to spend your whole life pretending?

Task Question 2   Is it possible for anyone to know you completely?

Questions to take you further

* How would they gain this complete knowledge of you?

* What does it mean to know someone completely?

* Can you be known without wanting to be?

* Can you be known better than you know yourself?

* If they knew you completely, could they ever be surprised, startled, confused, delighted, grateful, excited, etc. by the things you do?

* Is there anyone that ought to know us completely?

* Is your mind part of the world?

Task Question 3   Do we know ourselves completely?

Questions to take you further

* How do we gain knowledge of ourselves?

* Can we be wrong about ourselves?

* Do we have feelings that we don't know we have?

* Is it possible not to know your own thoughts? Do we have thoughts we are not aware of?

* Should we know ourselves completely?

* If we don't know ourselves, can we be held responsible for the things we do?

* To know ourselves do we need to know our pasts?

* Are we unknown or just unknowable?

The Soul

The soul is the human being considered as having a value in itself.

Simone Weil

You're in a foreign city killing time. The streets are frosty and you've got no money. Checking a map you decide to visit the Science Museum.

The building is a cross between a palace and a cathedral. You wander round looking at stuffed dead things and paint-chipped planets. You notice a woman sitting in a small tent draped in bunting. The sign on top reads 'The Greatest Discovery Science has Never Made'.

There's an empty chair facing her. She sees you and starts waving. Feeling vaguely interested you go over and sit down.

Her name badge says 'Scientific Philosopher'.

'Hello, Scientific Philosopher.'

'Hello,' she replies, sitting like a meerkat.

'So … what's the greatest discovery science has ever made?' you ask.

'*Milk!*' she says and bursts out laughing. Her cheeks turn red. 'Just kiddin', just kiddin',' she gasps, holding up her hand.

You watch her, still vaguely interested. Her face quickly straightens and she watches you back. It doesn't seem like she's going to answer your question.

'Okay, well what's the greatest discovery science has *never* made?'

Like a switch has been flicked, she cocks her head and starts talking.

'Science has the ability to look at the world with a power far greater than the naked eye. With the aid of microscopes and telescopes, science can see the extremely close and the incredibly far. We are now able to look deep inside the human body. We can see so far into the body we can almost see through it. We have seen all that there is to see. We have explored every corner. We have left no kidney stone unturned. We have found many things. But *what* haven't we found?

'We haven't found a soul.

'Inside the human organism there are blood cells. There is DNA. There are neurons in the brain – 86 billion of them. All this. But no soul. It's simply not there. The soul is the Greatest Discovery Science has Never Made.

'Why haven't we made it? Because you can't make something from nothing. The human organism has no soul.'

Her nostrils flare and she takes a breath.

Task Question 1   Has science proved that humans don't have souls?

Questions to take you further

* Can the soul be seen, heard, smelt, touched or tasted?

* Is the soul a type of object?

* Are there things that science can't know? Can science see everything?

* Is it possible to prove the absence of something?

* What would prove that we don't have souls?

* What are souls?

You nod sceptically. You're trying to find the right question when she starts up again.

'You may object that people talk about souls all the time. You may ask, "Does this mean they're just talking about nothing?" It would be a mistake to think so.

'When people say things like, "Bless your soul," or, "She's a kind soul," or, "That man has no soul," they're not talking about things that don't exist. No – what they really mean is along the lines of, "Thank you very much," and, "She's a kind person," and, "He's nasty and insensitive." That's what they really mean. They just have another way of putting it. It's like how we might describe someone as an angel. We don't literally mean he has wings and a halo. We just mean he's awfully nice and sweet.'

Task Question 2   When people talk about souls are they really talking about something else?

Questions to take you further

❖ When we speak of souls are we speaking literally?

❖ Could we translate all soul-speak into non-soul-speak?

❖ If we can't translate it, what are we talking about when we talk about souls?

❖ Do we have to believe in souls to talk of them?

❖ Does talking of them show that we believe in them?

❖ How could it be shown that we do have souls?

As an accompanying exercise, you could ask the class to look at examples of soul-speak and see if these can be translated into non-soul-speak. For example, Sylvia Plath's line from 'Kindness': 'What is so real as the cry of a child?/ A rabbit's cry may be wilder/ But it has no soul.' Or Emily Dickinson's, ' "Hope" is the thing with feathers –/ That perches in the soul.' Or Psalm 142, 'refuge failed me; no man cared for my soul … Bring my soul out of prison.' Or from Jack Kerouac's On the Road, *'the trucks roared, wham, and inside two minutes one of them cranked to a stop for me. I ran for it with my soul whoopeeing.'*

If these lines can have the souls translated out of them, it might entail the redundancy of such language, which leads into Task Question 3.

'And you know what,' she continues, 'we shouldn't mourn the loss of souls – not that they were there to begin with, mind you – because we don't even need them.

'Every day I talk to friends, I interact with people, I gossip. Never ever do I mention souls. I might say that my friend has a bad temper, or an excellent brain; I might describe them as happy, or sad, or silly. But in order to understand people I never talk about their souls. And this is true for most of us most of the time.

'It's something we hardly ever talk about, and that's because the word "soul" is a pretty useless word. It doesn't contribute to our knowledge or understanding of other people and why they do the things they do. We can understand people perfectly well without it.'

Task Question 3   Does the idea of the soul add to our understanding of other people?

Questions to take you further

* Do we need the idea of the soul?

* Could we do without it?

* Would it make a difference if the word was erased from our minds and every dictionary (see 'Erasure')?

Her expanding eyes are fixed on the cracked galaxy overhead. She's growing more excited. She's blinking like a hummingbird.

'And you know what else?' she says. 'In the future, like soon, when souls are a thing of the past, people, all of us, we're going to talk differently. We're not going to talk about things like sadness any more. We're going to talk about brains instead.

'Scientists have discovered that sadness is caused by having low levels of this stuff in the brain called serotonin. Serotonin is a neurotransmitter. When you have low levels of serotonin you become sad. When you have high levels you become happier. So our emotions are really just chemicals in the brain. And once everyone realises this, we won't even talk about sadness any more. We won't say, "I'm feeling sad today." We'll say, "Well darn, I have low serotonin levels today." We'll say that because that's what sadness really is. We won't need to talk about sadness any more.'

She looks down at you but the chair is empty. You've gone.

Task Question 4   Could talk of serotonin levels replace talk of sadness?

Questions to take you further

❖ Can we learn about ourselves by learning about the brain?

❖ Are emotions just chemicals in the brain?

❖ Is a person essentially their brain?

❖ Could we replace talk of people with talk of brains? Should, say, the National Rifle Association change their slogan to, 'Guns don't kill people, brains do'?

Gender

We're born naked, and the rest is drag.

RuPaul

Over the years the Ten Commandments have received a decent press. But within the Old Testament there are laws that are less widely known and somewhat stranger. For example, God tells us that we should not get tattoos, nor should we shave the sides of our heads, nor should we wear clothes which are a mix of wool and linen. He also tells us that we should never cross-dress. It is written:

A woman must not wear men's clothing, nor a man wear women's clothing, for the Lord your God detests anyone who does this.

Deuteronomy 22:5

Hermeneutic Question 1   What is meant by 'men's clothing' and 'women's clothing'?

This question is partly wondering whether clothes are essentially gendered, whether the distinction between men's and women's clothing is easily drawn. If underwear comes up, you might ask whether they think that's what God had in mind.

Starter Question 1   Why do men and women dress differently?

Questions to take you further

* Is it because our bodies are different?

* Is it because our identities are different?

* What are clothes for? Why do we all dress uniquely? What do our clothes say about us?

* Can clothes lie?

* If you lived on an island by yourself, would this affect how you dressed?

* Does our gender determine our clothes or do our clothes determine our gender?

- Are men and women wearing separate uniforms?

- Are there instances where men and women wear the same clothes? If so, does this mean that men are dressing as women, women as men, or both as neither?

- If men and women dress differently, why don't they also, say, eat different food?

In relation to this question, it might be interesting to wonder why, till the 1920s, young boys were dressed as girls. Why were they dressed like little women rather than little men? Why would they then start dressing like men after the age of 5 or so – what had changed? Are young boys closer to women than men? And why would it be considered abnormal to dress boys as girls today?

With the third bullet point, you could look at photographs of a variety of differently dressed people – the fashion blog 'The Sartorialist' is a good resource – and ask the class to transcribe, or translate, the clothes into first-person statements about the wearer's self/body/identity, e.g. 'I do not belong to my generation.'

Joan of Arc was a 15th century teenage knight who helped guide France to several victories over the English during the Hundred Years War. Believing she had been sent by God to drive the English out of France, she left home, refusing to marry the man her parents had chosen for her, and convinced the dauphin of her divine calling.

Dressed as a knight – she was not in disguise, not pretending to be a boy – in full armour, carrying her own banner, she led the army against the occupiers. Neither her gender nor her lowly status as an illiterate peasant stood in her way.

She was eventually captured, sold to the English and put on trial for heresy. It was her transvestism that particularly distressed the

Inquisition. Five of the 70 articles in the charges brought against her concerned her cross-dressing. One explains that she, 'entirely abandoned woman's clothes, with her hair cropped short and round in the fashion of young men, she wore shirt, breeches, doublet'. She had 'cast aside all womanly decency'. The judges saw this as a violation of natural law.

Asked why she dressed as a man, she said it was at the command of God and his angels. She was commanded to change into a dress, but she refused. She said she would rather die.

On 30 May 1431, at 19 years of age, she was burnt at the stake.

Hermeneutic Question 2   Why do you think God and the Inquisition were enraged by cross-dressing?

Questions to take you further

❖ Is it a violation of natural law?

❖ Do clothes help us summarise people? Do they lessen our confusion about people?

❖ Are clothes tied to status?

❖ Does God have a gender? If not, why is He so concerned about ours? What clothes does He wear?

❖ Should we be able to wear whatever we like? (For present-day sumptuary laws, see 'Democracy and Difference'.)

In the verse from Deuteronomy God is presuming that we all know our gender. If we didn't, we wouldn't know what to wear, and it would be unreasonable of God to detest us for breaking rules out of ignorance. So God must figure that we know what's what.

Let's imagine, then, that tomorrow men and women will wake up with no bodily differences and the spell which brings this about will also erase our memories.

Starter Question 2   Will we know our gender? Will we be able to follow God's commandment?

Questions to take you further

❖ Would you know by the things you liked?

❖ Would you know by the things you felt?

❖ Would you know by the way you thought?

❖ Would memories reveal your gender? Would all of them do so or only some of them?

❖ Would you still have a gender?

Draw a table with two columns: one headed, 'girl', the other, 'boy'. Then fill it with answers to the following question:

Starter Question 3   What are the differences between girls and boys?

After some time move from a table to a spectrum, with 'girls' at one end and 'boys' at the other, and ask the class where they would locate the tabled differences on this, and whether there are any absolute differences that belong at the extremes of the spectrum. There's no need to be bashful about the question; when bodily differences enter the discussion, cast them as just that: 'bodily differences'.

You might attempt to draw out the apparent differences by asking what gender different objects have, for example, the moon, sun, oak trees, poplars, mountains, the elements, clouds, snow, lava, clocks, etc.

Task Question 1   Does our gender define us?

Questions to take you further

❖ Is your gender an additional ingredient to your identity or does it affect everything about you?

- If you changed gender, would you still be you?
- Do we have to be either one gender or the other? Is it possible to be two things at once?
- Do the different genders experience the world differently?
- Can you imagine a third gender?
- Are genders defined by their mutual differences? Are they opposites?
- Could there have been only a single gender?

You can relate this back to the spectrum. If there are many qualities which were thought not to be absolutely 'girl' and not absolutely 'boy', you can ask whether it makes sense for individual people to be absolutely one or the other; that is, if we are composed of such qualities, and such qualities are not clearly defined, does that mean that we are not clearly defined? (i.e. is gender a vague or clear-cut concept?)

Task Question 2   Are we different because nature makes us that way or because society does?

Questions to take you further

- Are these differences essential or can they be changed?
- Are we defined by nature? Can we defy nature? Is it wrong to do so?
- Are we defined by society? Can we defy society? Is it wrong to do so?
- Are we taught how to be girls/boys or is it something that just happens?
- Why does society need to believe in these differences?
- Should these differences be maintained? Are they necessary for a good world?

❖ Who decides how things ought to be?

Suicide

That the sun will not rise tomorrow is no less intelligible a proposition,
and implies no more contradiction, than the affirmation, that it will rise.

David Hume

Starter Question 1   What is honour?

In 49 BC a civil war broke out in Rome that led to the ultimate fall of the Republic. The opposing forces were commanded by two mighty generals: Pompey the Great, who had the support of the Senate, and Julius Caesar, the official state enemy.

Pompey was assisted in his campaign by an important politician known as Cato the Younger. Cato had long been suspicious of Caesar, fearing that he harboured ambitions to overthrow the state. A strong believer in the Republic, Cato did not want Rome to find itself in the hands of an emperor. But Pompey's forces were defeated and the fallen general fled to Egypt where he was murdered. Caesar was declared dictator and the Roman Empire was born.

Cato refused to acknowledge or accept Caesar's authority and accordingly resolved to kill himself. Aware of his father's suicidal intentions, Cato's son stole his sword, but Cato flew into a rage, striking one of his servants and demanding the return of his weapon. The boy, unable to withstand his father's will, returned the sword. Cato scrutinised its sharp edge with satisfaction. 'Now I am my own master,' he said, and retired to bed with a book.

When he awoke to the dawn chorus, Cato removed the sword from its sheath and plunged it into his abdomen. In his death struggle he crashed loudly to the floor, arousing the attention of his servants. They rushed in to find Cato bleeding, bloody, still living, but close to death, and a doctor was called for. The doctor attempted to stitch the aperture but Cato, only half-conscious, became aware of the effort to save him. With a final gasp of strength he pushed the doctor aside, tore open the wound and died.

Cato's suicide was praised by Roman writers. Cicero, a contemporary, commended him for following his principles; his suicide was a testament to his character; it was a fitting act, an appropriate end. Decades later Seneca read of Cato's death with joy and excitement. He thought it was beautiful. To Seneca's eyes, Cato had given himself the freedom he was unable to give Rome, he had refused to be conquered. Reopening the wound, Cato had exhibited the courage to commit suicide not once, but twice, his hands accomplishing what the sword's steel could not. The suicide was an act of great honour.

Question to take you further

❖ Do you agree with Cicero and Seneca's view of Cato's death?

Oddly, the book Cato was reading on the eve of his suicide contained the thoughts of the Greek philosopher Socrates, who spoke against suicide. Socrates claimed that we are not our own possession and so we may not do to ourselves whatever we like. He also suggested that suicide is a form of running away. St Augustine echoed these thoughts when he criticised Cato for not being able to endure the shame of his defeat. Augustine also observed that Cato was quite happy to let his son live under Caesar's rule; he condemns Cato for letting his personal shame outweigh the love for his son.

Task Question 1   Is suicide honourable?

Questions to take you further

❖ Is suicidal immoral? Is it selfish?

❖ Is suicide irrational?

❖ Is suicide a right?

❖ Is suicide courage or cowardice (or neither)?

❖ Do we have a duty to live?

❖ Should suicide be illegal?

❖ Is life sacred?

Until 1961 suicide was illegal in the UK. One may wonder how such a crime can be punished and, if there is no available form of punishment, in what sense it is really a crime. The ancient Greek philosopher Plato suggested that people who commit suicide should be punished by being buried alone in unmarked graves (though suicide was legal in Athens and assistance was even offered).

In 18th century France, people who committed suicide were not even given this much. Their bodies were dragged through the streets face down and dumped on rubbish heaps. In England, the property of the deceased was confiscated by the government. And, in Russia, requests made in the will were ignored, the wishes of the dead were nullified.

Task Question 2   Is it possible to punish the dead?

Questions to take you further

- Do the dead have feelings? Do the dead care?
- Is the world of any importance to the dead?
- Do we have any duties towards the dead?
- Do the dead have responsibilities?
- Are the dead nihilists?
- Should the dead ever be punished?

Of course, some believe that punishment only really begins in death; the Task Question, however, is looking at whether you can punish the dead in the natural world.

Task Question 3   What makes life worth living?

Questions to take you further

- Is life always worth living?
- What are the things that life couldn't do without?

Typically Task Questions are closed questions, but here we have an exception. The first bullet point was an option, however, its emphasis is qualitatively different. Whereas the Task Question addresses what makes life good, the bulleted one tends towards the bad. That is, the actual Task Question encourages the pupils to think about what they want from life, and is on the side of appetite, whereas the bullet point is focused on deprivation, and though it works as a subsidiary question, it may be alienating if put centre-stage.

Understanding Death

We are two abysses – a well staring at the sky.

Fernando Pessoa

A student approached his wise teacher and asked, 'What is death?'

The teacher shrugged her shoulders and said, 'I don't know.'

'But you are a wise teacher.'

'Yes,' replied the teacher. 'But I am not a dead wise teacher.'

Hermeneutic Question   What is the teacher's point? Is it a good one?

Starter Question 1   What is death?

Questions to take you further

❖ Is death a something or a nothing?

❖ Is death an event?

❖ Is death an experience?

❖ Is death a weakness?

❖ Is death a limitation?

❖ Is death a part of life?

❖ When does death begin? Are we always dying?

❖ Are there experiences in life that are like death?

❖ What is life?

There are many accounts of animals apparently grieving in response to death. An African antelope, for example, was once observed seeming to mourn the death of its infant. The antelope had seen the infant killed and eaten by olive baboons. She chased the baboons away and stood staring at what was left of the body, remaining there motionless the entire night.

Elephants have also been seen to stand for days, with hanging ears and heads, over their stillborn babies. Orphan elephants who have witnessed their mothers being killed sometimes wake up making a screaming-like noise.

Magpies have been observed cackling in unison upon discovering the corpse of a fellow magpie, performing, you might think, a kind of avian requiem mass.

Task Question 1   Do animals understand death?

Questions to take you further

- Do animals understand ideas of existence, eternity and absence?

- Do animals understand that *they* will die? Do they understand that *others* will die?

- Is their understanding similar to ours?

- Is death the same for them as it is for us?

- Do we understand it better?

- How do they learn about it?

- Do animals know that they exist? What does it mean to know this?

- Can we understand animals?

Of course, it would be worth differentiating between animals, from caterpillars to chimpanzees. In running this Task Question, you can refer back to the Starter Question in order to clarify what the understanding of death involves. It might be worth enquiring whether, in order to understand death, you need to understand all the ideas evoked by the Starter Question and, for the next Task Question, whether there might be things about death that we do not, or cannot, know.

Imagine you were raised in a palace in a land of endless summer. The palace is built from marble that shines in the sun. The gardens are lined with orange trees; swimming pools stud the grounds like mirrors of the sky. Your clothes are woven from nature's softest materials. Jasmine can be smelt on the breeze that circles through the large palace rooms. You are given everything you ask for. When you were three you asked for a zoo and it was given to you. You have grown up with your animals, with your tiger, giraffe, your marmot and flamingo. Servants occupy the palace, tending lovingly to your needs. Your parents are always happy to be with you and they make no demands of you. But in all this time, in this first 15 years of your life, you have never travelled beyond the palace walls, and no one within the palace has died, nor has anyone ever told you about death, indeed, 'death' is a word you do not know, it has never been used in your presence.

Starter Question 2   Would you know about death?

Questions to take you further

- Would you know that others die?

- Would you know that you will die?

- Can we know about things we don't have the words for?

- Is it possible not to know about death?

- If we do know about it, where does this knowledge come from?

- Does aging imply death?

Answers may be given to the effect that you would have seen flowers, plants or insects die. There are a couple of ways to take this. You can either 'if' your way back to the Starter Question – 'And if you hadn't seen such things, would you know ... ' – or you can ask whether the mortality of yourself and others can be inferred from the deaths of non-human beings (as encountered in the 'Time' session, Borges once wrote that everyone runs the risk of being the first immortal, suggesting that our mortality cannot even be inferred from the deaths of other people).

The early part of the life of the Buddha is believed to have resembled this enclosure of luxury. He too was ignorant of many things, but when, as a young man, he left the palace for the first time, he witnessed sickness, aging and death. Before this he had not known that the world was imbued with such suffering and the reality pained him. Following this experience he decided he would use his life to search for an end to suffering.

According to the story of Buddha's early life, death was something he learnt about only once he was already a young man. Some have claimed, however, that death isn't something we discover, but something we are born knowing.

Psychoanalysis is the study of secrets. It tells us that there are areas within us, parts of our minds, which contain thoughts and desires that we are not conscious of; we live them, but we don't know them. Sigmund Freud, the first psychoanalyst, claimed that one of the secret things inside us is a 'death instinct'. He claimed that since all life awoke from lifeless matter – since we are composed of inanimate stuff – there is an instinct hidden within us to return to this state of inanimate lifelessness. The knowledge of death is a part of our very nature. It is in our blood. Later psychoanalysts followed Freud by claiming that babies are born fearing death. This is why they cry; they are fighting their innate knowledge of death.

Task Question 2   Is the idea of death something we are born with or something we learn?

Questions to take you further

❖ If we learn it, when and how do we do so?

❖ If it is not learnt through real examples, how is it learnt?

❖ Do infants have a different idea of death to the rest of us?

❖ Do we understand it better?

❖ If the idea is there from birth, how does it get there?

❖ Is having an instinct of death the same as having an understanding of it?

❖ Do we understand death?

Is death bad? The German philosopher Arthur Schopenhauer thought that death is what keeps us alive. If we were not afraid of death, if the destruction of the body did not terrify us, he suggests many of us may have already chosen to die. Schopenhauer is here echoing Shakespeare's Hamlet:

For in that sleep of death what dreams may come,
When we have shuffled off this mortal coil,
Must give us pause. There's the respect
That makes Calamity of so long life.

Others have thought of death as more than a deterrent. Seneca, a Roman writer, believed that death gives us the courage to live well;

living with death in mind can strengthen us to illness and misfortune; being well-prepared can soften our suffering.

The German philosopher Martin Heidegger argued that living with an awareness of our own death makes us truer to ourselves; it leads us to see that we are responsible for our own lives, that we have a life and it is ours to live. The awareness of death awakens us to the realisation that nothing is set in stone, nothing is permanent, nothing has to be the way it is, therefore we are free to live in our own way. The awareness of death brings a fullness to life.

Albert Camus, on the other hand, insisted that death is simply bad. It doesn't free us, it limits us. It is a despicable infringement. But this doesn't mean we should ignore it. A good life, Camus claimed, is one that is lived despite death. To live with an awareness of death is the best we can do to defy it, it is the best life on offer. We should not be defeated by the thought of death nor should we pretend that it isn't real. We should stare the thought down and live. To live as defiance is the way to happiness.

Task Question 3   Is death bad?

Questions to take you further

- ❖ Is immortality preferable?
- ❖ Is our death relevant to our life?
- ❖ Is an awareness of death good for us?
- ❖ Are we better off not thinking about death?
- ❖ Is death unfair?
- ❖ Is death the worst thing that can happen to us?
- ❖ Is it a tragedy?
- ❖ Is it bad to be nothing?

You may prefer to present the Task Question before the philosophical summaries in order not to pre-empt the pupils' own thinking. This structure of things needn't make a waste of the summaries; they can be introduced after the discussion, then the Task Question can be recycled with a new talk time. Recycling a Task Question is sometimes a useful way of refreshing an enquiry.

Some might say that death is not bad because it marks the beginning of the afterlife, but religious differences need not preclude a discussion. The way round it is simply to treat these differences hypothetically: 'So, if there is an afterlife, does that mean that death isn't bad?' or 'If there is no afterlife, is death bad?' This treatment is a way of exploring the philosophical relationship between the afterlife and the value of death; it turns the straightforward assertion of a belief into a starting point for philosophical awareness.

Freedom

Your boundaries are your quest.

Rumi

The ancient Greek story of Icarus tells of a girl who got carried away.

Icarus and her mother, Daedalus, were being kept captive on the island of Crete by King Minos. Their memories of home were becoming faint and diluted with time. Daedalus could feel the magnetic pull of her past exerting its force from across the waters and she longed to return, but Minos had blocked the way by sea.

Daedalus was an inventor – it was her business to turn absurdities into realities. Though land and water were closed, the air remained open. She set to work crafting two sets of human wings. The wings, though soft, ethereal like dreams, were vast in span, wild and strong, like the wings of an albatross. Icarus marvelled at their construction, a collusion of wax and feathers; the growing substance of adventure.

The fugitives would not have an opportunity to rehearse the wings because the king's sentinels were always at their posts. Their first flight would be their final attempt. When the day came to take the leap, the skies were clear and the air was still.

Daedalus fastened the wings to Icarus' arms. 'I warn you,' she said. 'You must follow a course midway between heaven and earth. If you fly too high, the sun will melt the wax. If you fly too low, the water will soak your feathers. You must fly halfway between the two. Do you understand?'

'I understand,' Icarus said.

'I am your guide. You must follow me.'

'I will.'

They stood poised at the edge of a precipice with their eyes forwards and fears below. Nudged by some mysterious impulse their feet leapt free of the ground, they gave two flaps of their wings and flew into the blue.

As the shadows of human birds crossed the earth's surface, workers stopped to squint above. Shepherds, fishermen and farmers took a moment to watch the passing glamour.

The girl Icarus began to enjoy the thrill of swooping boldly through the air. Forgetting where she was escaping to or what she was escaping from, she became absorbed in the escape itself. Drawn on by the bliss of open sky she left her guide and lifted higher, breaking the clouds and soaring, till she came too close to the blazing sun. The wax that bound her wings together softened and streamed off into the void.

Icarus moved her naked arms up and down, but featherless they had no grasp of the air. She felt her body plummeting and cried her mother's name louder and louder till her lungs were flooded with salt water and she sank unconscious to the bottom of the sea.

Daedalus looked round and felt dizzy at the seamless absence.

'Icarus! Icarus! Where are you?' she called, as a scattering of feathers lay on the water's surface.

I've flipped the traditional genders. Flip them back, if you like.

Hermeneutic Question   Does the story have a moral? Is it a good moral?

Questions to take you further

❖ Was Icarus arrogant? Was she a fool? Did she deserve to die?

❖ Is there such a thing as too much confidence?

❖ Is there such a thing as too much pleasure?

❖ Is getting carried away a virtue?

❖ Do parents know best?

❖ What is an ideal parent? Are they infallible protectors?

❖ Who's to blame: Daedalus, Icarus, the sun or something else?

❖ William Blake wrote, 'You never know what is enough unless you know what is more than enough.' Is this true?

You may or may not want to include this preamble:

Icarus discovered a pleasure unavailable to humans. She was buoyed, untrammelled by gravity, the earth's mass, free of the human incapacity to travel beyond the body's muscle. Without the use of force or fuel, flying with feathers, not in defiance of physics, but in communion with it, with grace not might, Icarus soared free and embodied. Her wings were not a narrow tunnel to her freedom but the joyous fulfilment of it.

Task Question 1   We cannot fly. Does this mean we are not free?

Questions to take you further

* Does freedom mean having no limits?

* Does freedom mean being able to do whatever we want?

* Are human beings limited?

* Was Icarus free?

* In a way, Icarus disobeyed both nature and her mother. Do we need to break the rules to be free?

* Is freedom good?

* Are we free?

* Why is flight a perennial object of desire?

You could look at this final question in relation to Yves Klein as well as Icarus; they both struggled poignantly with flight. Having discussed the Hermeneutic Question, show the class Klein's picture, Leap into the Void, *and ask: 'Does this picture have a moral?' Klein's photograph is a composite image, a so-called fake. In reality there were people standing ready to catch him. But he was depicting something he believed he had actually achieved. He believed he was capable of levitation, even flight. His wife said he was sure of it. Yet no one ever witnessed these acts, and his attempts to repeat them before his disbelieving friends resulted only in sore bones. Two years after the picture was taken Klein died of a heart attack.*

The Icarean image of flight as getting carried away is echoed in Dante's Inferno, *where in the second circle of hell the lustful – 'those who make reason slave to appetite' – are seen 'like cranes in flight' battling the winds. But in Psalm 55 flight is an image of asylum: 'Oh that I had wings like a dove! for then I would fly away, and be at rest.' Considering these different conceptions of human flight, you could pursue the question of whether it is better to stay earthbound, purposeful and strong, or whether it is better to exchange the will for wings, to abandon effort and strength and be carried by our evanescent wishes. It's hard not to be figurative about this, but the question could be framed as: would you rather live as a leaf in the wind or a trout fighting the current? And which of these two options presents the truer image of freedom?*

Again, the preamble is optional.

One moral that may be taken from the story is that there is such a thing as too much freedom; that freedom in excess endangers us. Moderation, balance, prudence … we might take Icarus' early death to be a lesson on the necessity of wisdom. Not too close to the water or too near to the sun: we must stay well-centred, followers of the middle way; better to ensure survival than flirt with freedom. Perhaps the story is telling us – and we may wonder how much freedom it gives us in making up our own minds about this – that yes, we ought to be free, but sensibly so.

Task Question 2   Is it possible to be too free?

Questions to take you further

❖ Should you be free to say what you want?

❖ Should you be free to marry who you want?

❖ Should you be free to do whatever you want to your body?

❖ Should you be free not to care about others?

❖ Should you be free not to work?

❖ What makes freedom excessive?

❖ Does the idea of moderate freedom make sense?

❖ Should we all, in some form or another, be wearing chains?

❖ Can we be both compliant and free?

* Are we only really free once we have discovered what it means to be *too* free?

Task Question 3   Does school take away your freedom?

Questions to take you further

* Do you need education?
* Do needs take away your freedom?
* Should you be free not to go to school?
* Does education free you?
* Can you be forced to be free?
* Is school more like the wings or the sun in the story of Icarus?
* Calculators have made mental arithmetic somewhat pointless. Can you imagine a device that would make all education pointless?
* What is the point of education?

Responsibility

I choose being born.

Jean-Paul Sartre

Starter Question   What is responsibility?

Questions to take you further

* Are children responsible for their actions?
* Are animals responsible for theirs?
* Are we responsible for our dreams?

❖ Are we responsible for our desires?

❖ Does responsibility imply culpability?

❖ What does it mean to say we are responsible for ourselves?

❖ What does it mean to say we are responsible for others?

Below is a thought experiment, a hypothetical situation that can help to crystallise our thoughts on a given topic. It is sometimes necessary to explain the differences between a thought experiment and a story. It should be emphasised that the point is not to try and resolve the particular situation, but to accept the terms of the situation as a means of discovering our general ideas. In the following case, the point is not to try and save all the patients, but to use the artificial scenario to explore our ideas about desert and responsibility. Thought experiments can be ludicrously contrived, to the extent that they distort rather than focus our thoughts; it could be the case that this applies to the following one, so if a pupil objects to the pretence, they may be on to something.

Imagine an understaffed hospital in a remote area of a distant country. The hospital has only three patients: two with cancer and one with heart disease. Patient 1's cancer is the result of years of smoking, patient 2's cancer is hereditary and patient 3 suffered a cardiac arrest while training as an Olympic rower. Both the smoker and the rower knew of the danger they faced. Patient 1 was perfectly aware of the dangers of smoking and patient 3 had been warned that rowing could complicate her pre-existing heart condition.

These are the hospital's only patients, but there is a problem. The hospital is not equipped with the resources to give each patient the surgery they require. Only one patient will be able to receive the appropriate treatment. The other two will most certainly die.

Task Question 1 You are the hospital administrator. Which of the three patients would you save?

Questions to take you further

- Is the smoker responsible for their illness?

- Is the rower responsible for her cardiac arrest?

- Are the smoker's choices similar to the rower's?

- Which patient is the biggest victim?

- Are there factors besides need that determine desert?

- Is smoking wrong?

In the summer of 2011, a man was shot dead in Tottenham, north London, by police officers. The man's friends and relatives marched to Tottenham Police Station demanding that the police account for their actions. Crowds gathered, frustration grew and a riot started. Buildings were torched, shops looted and cars damaged. The following day rioting occurred in other areas of London, and two days later, riots were taking place in cities throughout England. Shops were broken into, money stolen, stock emptied, the police were attacked, fires were started and five people died. In total over 3,000 arrests were made and in London alone the damage is estimated to have exceeded £300 million.

Of those who were brought before the courts, 90% were male and half were under the age of 21 (source: http://www.bbc.co.uk/news/uk-15426720). Three-quarters had a previous conviction or caution. Some 42% of the schoolchildren arrested received free school meals (compared to the national average of 16%) and two-thirds were classed as having special educational needs (compared to the national average of 21%). Of the adults, 35% were claiming out-of-work benefits (compared to the national average of 12%).

The rioters, as well as being more educationally disadvantaged and more punished than most, were also, on average, poorer. But

Prime Minister David Cameron denounced the claim that poverty was a factor:

Now the fires have been put out and the smoke has cleared, the question hangs in the air: why? These riots were not about race. These riots were not about government cuts. And these riots were not about poverty – that would insult the millions of people who, whatever the hardship, would never dream of making people suffer like this.

No, this was about behaviour: people showing indifference to right and wrong, people with a twisted moral code, people with a complete absence of self-restraint.

Responsibility for crime always lies with the criminal. These people were all volunteers, they didn't have to do what they did, and they must suffer the consequences. I've said before that there is a major problem in our society with children growing up not knowing the difference between right and wrong. This is not about poverty, it is about culture. A culture that glorifies violence, that shows disrespect to authority, that says everything about rights but nothing about responsibilities. Restoring a stronger sense of responsibility across our society, in every town, in every street, in every estate, is something I'm determined to do.

Elsewhere Cameron said that the riots were 'criminality, pure and simple' – words that strangely echo George Bush Snr's from the 1992 LA riots: 'What we saw last night is not about civil rights … it's been the brutality of a mob, pure and simple.' As a comparison or tangent, the LA riots – starting as they did with the attack on Rodney King – could also be worth considering.

Hermeneutic Question   What does Cameron mean by, 'Responsibility for the crime always lies with the criminal'?

Questions to take you further

- ❖ This is a claim he asserts but doesn't argue for. What reasons could he give to justify his point?

- ❖ What is Cameron's explanation for the riots?

Task Question 2   Were the rioters to blame for the damage they caused?

Questions to take you further

- ❖ Are the rioters victims (did their circumstances make them riot) or responsible agents?

- ❖ Is being blameworthy for the damage the same thing as being responsible for it?

- ❖ What would make people want to riot?

- ❖ Is society to blame for the damage caused?

- ❖ Is society responsible for the damage caused?

- ❖ Is there always someone to blame?

- ❖ Are people responsible for their poverty? If they aren't, who is?

- ❖ Does Cameron's corrective sound credible?

Thinking

Is there such a thing as silence?

John Cage

Starter Question   What is thinking?

Questions to take you further

❖ What motivates thought?

❖ Is thinking a choice? Is it a pleasure?

❖ Are there thoughts we should be punished for thinking?

❖ How would you describe to an outsider what is happening when you are thinking?

❖ Is thinking like playing your mind in the way fingers play a piano?

❖ Is thinking different to daydreaming?

❖ What does, 'I'm *trying* to think,' mean? What is stopping us? How do we overcome it?

❖ 'I'll be thinking of you.' Why is this reassuring?

❖ Do we have control over our thoughts?

❖ Are thoughts unspoken sentences? Are thoughts composed of words? If not, what are they composed of?

❖ Do we need a voice in order to think?

❖ Do fake people have fake thoughts? Do our thoughts perfectly reflect who we are?

❖ Does every action require thought? Is thinking a kind of action?

❖ Where do thoughts come from?

❖ Is there anything that exists in the mind prior to thought?

❖ If someone didn't know how to think, would it be possible to teach them?

Excuse the barrage. One way to use these questions would be to treat them as Task Questions, but without a talk time, and with only a minute given to each one, boarding the answers to build a mind-map as you go. This whiplash approach may do something to convey the spiralling strangeness of thinking (and philosophy needn't be slow).

A few hundred years ago, René Descartes shut himself in a room and tried to discover what he was. After meditating on the existence of himself and the world, he came to uncover, as he understood it, the true and essential basis of his being. He believed that he was essentially a mind and that thinking was the fundamental basis of his existence. If he did not think, his existence would be in jeopardy. He wrote:

... thought; this alone is inseparable from me. I am, I exist – that is certain. But for how long? For as long as I am thinking. For it could be that were I totally to cease from thinking, I should totally cease to exist.

Task Question 1   Do we need to think to exist?

Questions to take you further

❖ Are we always thinking?

❖ If we lost our thoughts, what else would we lose about ourselves?

❖ If we stopped thinking, what else would we stop doing?

❖ Is it possible to think somebody else's thoughts? How can you tell that your thoughts are yours?

❖ If someone could read your mind, would they know you completely? Can minds be read?

❖ Do we know that other people are thinking? Do we know that they exist?

❖ How do we know that we are thinking? How do we know that we exist?

❖ Are we our minds? Do we live in our minds?

❖ What does Descartes mean by, 'cease to be'? Is ceasing to be a bad thing?

❖ What is inseparable from us?

Is there value in thinking? Hannah Arendt – whom I shall call a philosopher by telling you that she refused to be called one – believed that thinking is the quintessence of being alive. She characterised thinking as a force of destruction. Thinking sweeps through the mind and destabilises everything we know and understand. The prefix 'I think' conveys doubt because thinking is a solvent of certainty. It is an endless search for meaning, a *desirous* questioning that is never satisfied. 'What? Why? Where? How?' – these are questions that erode their answers. Thinking is restlessness, disorientation and instability.

Thinking wakes us up, it brings us to life. Non-thinking is sleepwalking. A life of non-thinking would be meaningless. If we do not think, if we don't turn inwards, we can easily become enlisted in evil. Thinking is a basis of conscience, a prerequisite for judgement.

Arendt's account of thinking is seemingly at odds with that of Zen Buddhism. At the heart of Zen philosophy is the idea of *wu-nien*, meaning, no-thought. Whereas Arendt sees action as the essence of the mind, Zen believes in the value of passivity. 'What? Why? Where?

How?' – these questions are a curse and they are irrelevant to our understanding life.

Wu-nien involves having thoughts and yet not having them. We needn't empty our mind, but we should not actively pursue thinking. We should live effortlessly, in a state of 'no-mind-ness', for the restlessness of the active mind will award us no peace.

According to Zen, no-thought enables simplicity, the ability to live without being hounded by the incessant activities of the mind. We should not judge experience. We should not pursue meaning. We should act straightforwardly, silencing the *neediness* of thoughts. Action rather than thought is the basis of living.

Task Question 2   Do you agree with Arendt or Zen?

Questions to take you further

❖ Is there a limit to how much we should think?

❖ 'She is a mindless person, very thoughtless indeed.' Could this be a good thing?

❖ Is it possible not to think?

❖ Is life essentially confusing? Does it require thought?

❖ Does understanding require thought?

❖ Are Arendt and Zen opposites?

❖ Who would have the better life: the Arendt-thinker or the Zen-thinker?

❖ If you agree with Zen, should you be thinking about this?

Agree/disagree questions can impose artificial polarities on a topic, but when the class isn't divided into sides (as in a debate) this needn't be a concern. In this context, agree/disagree questions can help focus the class's thoughts on the given topic, and through finding that their views do not fall squarely into either camp, they come to see for themselves the variety of possible views, and that their thoughts are their own, distinct and not easily assimilated into those of others.

Language and Originality

I am convinced that I can not exaggerate enough even to lay the foundation of a true expression.

Henry Thoreau

A poetry anthology was published in the 1960s which contained an entry by a writer called Aram Saroyan. In the centre of a blank white page the entry consisted of just this:

lighght

The anthology Saroyan's piece featured in was government (taxpayer) funded. Many politicians were appalled to find what the public's money was being used to support. One congressman (William Scherle, a Republican) is reported to have said, 'If my kid came home from school spelling like that, I would have stood him in the corner with a dunce cap.'

Starter Question 1   Is it a poem?

Questions to take you further

- If it's not a poem, what is it? Is it a word? A sentence?
- Is it meaningful?
- Do poems have rules they must follow? Who decides these rules?
- What do we want from poems?
- If it were a typo, would it remain a poem?

- Could there be a language with which it is impossible to write poetry?

- What is a poem?

With each of these Starter Questions, the responses will form an answer to the bottom bullet point. To that end, you can mind-map the responses as you take them.

The Irish writer James Joyce once wrote a very famous book that almost no one has read. Some call it a masterpiece. He called it *Finnegans Wake.* Here's an extract:

Come on, ordinary man with that large big nonobli head, and that blanko berbecked fischial ekksprezzion Machinsky Scapolopolos, Duzinascu or other. Your machelar's mutton leg's getting musclebound from being too pulled. Noah Beery weighed stone thousand one when Hazel was a hen. Now her fat's falling fast. Therefore, chatbags, why not yours? There are 29 sweet reasons why blossomtime's the best.

Starter Question 2   Is this language?

Questions to take you further

- If it isn't language, what is it?

- Is it English? What makes language English?

- Does it make sense? Is it meaningful?

- Does language have rules it has to follow? Who decides these rules?

- Is there such a thing as correct English?

- ❖ What do we want from language?
- ❖ Does language have to be meaningful?
- ❖ Could you make up your own private language?
- ❖ What is language?

There was a revolution in poetry not so long ago. Poetic form had traditionally been governed by patterns of metre and rhyme. For example:

We have but faith: we cannot know;
For knowledge is of things we see;
And yet we trust it comes from Thee,
A beam of darkness: let it grow.

This is the English poet Tennyson writing in iambic tetrameter with an ABBA rhyme scheme. The lines move to four lots of ti-tums, with the final words of the first and last lines rhyming, and so too the middle lines. This arrangement repeats itself across 133 stanzas in Tennyson's poem, *In Memoriam*.

That is how things tended to be. But it changed with the American, Walt Whitman's, *Leaves of Grass*. Whitman did not write in repetition with predetermined rules of rhyme. He wrote like this:

I celebrate myself,
And what I assume you shall assume,
For every atom belonging to me as good belongs to you.

I loafe and invite my soul,

I lean and loafe at my ease ... observing a spear of summer grass.

Houses and rooms are full of perfumes ... the shelves are crowded with perfumes,
I breathe the fragrance myself, and know it and like it,
The distillation would intoxicate me also, but I shall not let it.

The atmosphere is not a perfume ... it has no taste of the distillation ... it is odorless,
It is for my mouth forever ... I am in love with it,
I will go to the bank by the wood and become undisguised and naked,
I am mad for it to be in contact with me.

Whereas traditional forms of poetry are rule-bound, Whitman was writing in free verse. Traditional forms observe fixed patterns of metre and rhyme; free verse abandons these rules. It has no strict adherence to metre or rhyme. Whitman's language wanders freely, leaving the train-tracks for the wind.

Though traditional forms conceive of language as a medium from which a poem is carved, free verse takes language as something you manipulate and mould in order to articulate the poem your mind is hankering after. For traditional forms, language holds an authority over us, it is larger than us and we must abide by its rules. In free verse, language follows us, we bring it to life and our thoughts are its energy. We don't use language so much as invent it.

Are there laws that govern free verse? D. H. Lawrence wrote, 'externally applied law would be mere shackles and death. The law must come new each time from within.' Language is something *we* speak, it does

not speak us. The laws are our own. The American poet Robert Frost thought that this was all well and good, but free verse, he said, is like playing tennis with the net down.

Task Question 1   Is language something you conform to or something you invent?

Questions to take you further

❖ Are our thoughts limited to our language? Can we think beyond language?

❖ Are we trapped by language? Can we communicate beyond language?

❖ Does language require rules? Do these rules jeopardise our freedom?

❖ Is free verse really free?

❖ Is a rule really a rule if, as Lawrence suggests, you make it by yourself, for yourself?

❖ Do we choose our first language?

❖ Does America have its own language?

❖ Is language information? Is it music?

❖ Should language make sense? Is it lucid like a road sign or moving and confusing like a dream?

❖ What do you think Frost meant by his tennis quip?

Before focusing on the philosophy, it would be good to present a few more of the Tennyson stanzas and then ask the class whether they prefer free or traditional verse.

Jean-Paul Sartre's *Nausea* is the fictional diary of a 30-year-old character named Antoine Roquentin. Living alone in a small seaside town in France, Roquentin starts to suffer from a mood that swells inside him and the world gradually dissolves. He begins to sense that life is random, pointless, meaningless, an accident. The mood takes him arbitrarily. He might be sitting in a café, walking down a street or working on his book. Suddenly he will feel that there is no reason for anything. Everything is nothing and the world is spectral.

One evening, sitting on a park bench amid the trees, feeling tired and suffocated, Roquentin undergoes a powerful revelation:

I was in the municipal park just now. The root of the chestnut tree plunged into the ground just underneath my bench. I no longer remembered that it was a root. Words had disappeared, and with them the meaning of things, the methods of using them, the feeble landmarks which men have traced on their surface.

Existence had suddenly unveiled itself. The root, the park gates, the bench, the sparse grass on the lawn, all that had vanished; the diversity of things, their individuality, was only an appearance, a veneer. This veneer had melted, leaving soft, monstrous masses, in disorder – naked, with a frightening, obscene nakedness.

Hermeneutic Question   What has just happened to Roquentin?

Questions to take you further

- ❖ What is the veneer?
- ❖ Why does he now perceive a disordered mass? How does it relate to the disappearance of words?
- ❖ Why does he refer to words as 'feeble landmarks'?
- ❖ What is his view of language?

Task Question 2 Do you agree with Roquentin? Does language prevent us from seeing the world as it really is?

Questions to take you further

❖ Does language reflect the world or does it shape it? Is it more like a mirror or a cookie cutter?

❖ Can we understand the world without language?

❖ How many things in this room lack words?

❖ What does 'the world as it really is' mean? Is there such a thing?

❖ If we can only ever see the world through our own eyes, does that mean we can never really see the world?

❖ Is it possible to step outside of ourselves and view the world? Can we see a tree without seeing it as a *tree*?

❖ Is Roquentin's view of language tied to his view of life?

❖ Do people who speak different languages experience the world differently?

Both Task Questions are wondering whether language is alienating. The first wonders whether language alienates us from ourselves, the second whether it alienates us from the world.

Autonomy

I do not do what I want, but I do the very thing I hate.

St Paul

On a spring evening in 1977, Francine Hughes poured gasoline round the bed where her ex-husband, Mickey Hughes, lay sleeping. She struck a match and the bed ignited. Flames spread throughout the house and Mickey was killed. Francine drove to the county jail and cried, 'I did it! I did it! I did it!' but she was never punished. The jury at her trial declared her not guilty by reason of temporary insanity.

For 12 years Mickey had mistreated Francine. He was frequently violent towards her, prevented her from seeing her family and friends and threatened to kill her if she ever left him. When she was pregnant with their fourth child, Francine followed the advice of a social worker and filed for divorce. But Mickey would not leave her alone. After suffering severe injuries in a car accident, he was helpless and Francine took on the responsibility of caring for him. They started living together again.

On the day of his death, Mickey had attacked Francine and burnt the books she was using to study for a secretarial course. He had told her he would take a sledgehammer to her car so she would be unable to drive to college. That evening she thought of escape. She imagined taking the children and driving, never turning back. She had dreamt of doing this for many years, but on this night she decided to act.

While waiting for her son to return home so they could leave together, Francine reflected on the past 12 years of her life and she was filled with anger. She suddenly wanted to erase it all, her whole life with Mickey, and burn everything. Holding a can of gasoline she entered the bedroom where Mickey was sleeping. A voice in her mind whispered, 'Do it! Do it! Do it!'

On trial later that year, the court was told by a clinical psychologist that Francine had been 'overwhelmed by the massive onslaughts of her most primitive emotions. Emotions she had suppressed for so many years overwhelmed her. … She experienced a breakdown of her psychological processes so that she was no longer able to utilise judgement … no longer able to control her impulses … unable to prevent herself from acting in the way she did.'

A psychiatrist added that Francine was 'unable to form a criminal intent because she lacked the capacity to appreciate the difference between right and wrong', and she had been 'temporarily out of control'.

The jury ruled that Francine was temporarily insane at the time of Mickey's death and she was acquitted.

Hermeneutic Question   Was Mickey Hughes murdered?

Questions to take you further

* If Mickey's death wasn't the result of an intentional action, does that mean it was an accident?

* If Francine's actions lacked (criminal) intent, does that mean she didn't really perform those actions?

* Did Francine choose to strike the match or was she made to?

* If Francine's actions were not intentional, could it be that it was another 'false' part of her that intentionally performed the actions?

* If she acted out of a desire to kill, does that mean she acted intentionally?

* Should Francine have been punished? Should she feel guilty?

* Does it make sense to speak of animals or plants as murdering each other?

Task Question 1   Is it possible to lose self-control?

Questions to take you further

- When we have self-control, what are we controlling?

- When we lose self-control, what is controlling us?

- Is it possible to have total self-control?

- Are most actions the result of our self-control?

- Are we often out of control?

- Are out-of-control actions meaningful?

- Is self-control good?

The testifying psychiatrist at the trial argued that Francine's arson was not premeditated because it was 'not in her character to plan something with such a degree of violence' and 'something like this would be abhorrent to her if she thought about it in advance'. The implication appears to be that since violence was out of character for Francine, so too was the killing of Mickey; it did not arise from Francine's real self but from a corrupted aberrant version of her self.

Task Question 2   Is there such a thing as a 'real self'?

Questions to take you further

- Is our real self revealed in our plans or in our spontaneous actions?

- Is it possible not to be who we are?

- Is it possible to betray ourselves? Is it bad to?

- Oscar Wilde wrote, 'One's real life is so often the life that one does not lead.' What does this mean?

- Are all parts of our self equally real?

- How can we recognise our real self?

- Can our real self change?

❖ If we can individually lose our real self, can we collectively, as a society, lose our real self?

❖ Was it Francine's real self that struck the match?

Mind and Body

Physiological life is of course not 'Life'. And neither is psychological life. Life is the world.

Ludwig Wittgenstein

This session starts with a game of Pictionary. Split the class into two groups. The cards you give to participants from the first group will not only contain the word of the object they must depict, but also a list of objects they must not depict. They are not allowed to draw anything bodily: no eyes, mouths, hands, etc. The second group can draw what they like. Thirty seconds for each attempt will do.

Words for the first group	Words for the second group
1. Joy	1. Joy
2. Thinking	2. Sadness
3. Ghost	3. Kindness
4. Sadness	4. Ghost
5. Anger	5. Thinking

Hermeneutic Question 1 Do the results of the game reveal anything of philosophical interest?

I have it played out that the second group will win and this will demonstrate either our essentially embodied nature or the essentially embodied meaning of our words. But I could be wrong: the first group may win and the class may draw altogether different philosophical conclusions. Don't steer them towards any particular interpretation of the results. Let them make of it what they will.

'Somatophobia' was invented in the 20th century though somatophobia is apparently much older. It is an affliction or attitude characterised by fear and hostility towards the body. Plato, for example, believed that our pure self, our soul, is 'crippled by its partnership with the body'. He said that though we can glimpse the semblance of perfect Beauty in other people, it is 'cluttered up with human flesh and colours and a great mass of mortal rubbish'. 'Life in the body is of itself an evil,' summarised Plotinus, a follower of Plato.

St Paul's writings in the Bible similarly speak of his wish to be rescued from his body, because 'those who are in the realm of the flesh cannot please God … the mind governed by the flesh is death'. Part of the wonder of God is that one day He will change our 'vile' bodies.

John Calvin, another influential Christian, was so appalled by the body that he forbade dancing. Our true life is our afterlife, when the elect will be released from the 'prison-house of the body', no longer bound by the 'fetters of the body'.

Task Question 1   Is the body a prison?

Questions to take you further

❖ Is somatophobia rational?

❖ Are permanent things more beautiful than changing things?

❖ Is our mind in conflict with our body?

❖ Are the bad things we do more a result of the body or the mind? Do bodies make us bad?

❖ Is it better to live for the mind or the body?

Tithonus, the brother of Priam, king of Troy, was gorgeous. Eos, the Goddess of Dawn, fell in love with him and took him away to live with her, but she knew that, unlike her, he would someday die. To ensure they would always be together, Eos asked Zeus to make Tithonus immortal, which Zeus did, but when Eos asked for his immortality she forgot to ask for eternal youth, and so Tithonus lived forever but aged eternally. By his 200th birthday he was already shrunken and frail, unable to speak or move, and this was only the beginning of his cruel immortality. Eos, after aeons, eventually became too bored of caring for the ever-shrivelling man and locked him in a room where he turned into a cicada.

Though Tithonus had defied death he had not escaped time. His eternal life was burdened by the frailties of a decaying body. If only Tithonus had had WiFi …

Futurologists – scholars of the future – have suggested that by 2050 we will have the opportunity to live forever, without the nuisance of a body, by uploading our minds to a machine. All the information contained in our brains will be digitally transferred to a supercomputer and we will live forever in virtual online environments. This is known as digital immortality. The former-head of the futurology department at BT has speculated that young people today may never die. They will have the opportunity to do what Tithonus could not; by discarding their bodies and escaping time, they will live agelessly forever.

Hermeneutic Question 2   Is this prediction realistic?

Questions to take you further

- Is the mind like a computer? Are we like machines?

- Are memories information?

- Are computers like minds? Do computers have memories? Do they have a past?

- Is immortality possible?
- Is the idea of digital immortality a religious or scientific one?
- Would you want digital immortality?
- Is it possible to be a scholar of the future?

Task Question 2   Does the idea of a disembodied existence make sense?

Questions to take you further

- Hell is thought to be painful. Is pain possible without a body?
- Heaven is thought to be pleasurable. Is pleasure possible without a body?
- What does it mean to talk of a 'suffering soul'?
- If we've never experienced disembodiment, where does the idea come from?
- Is dreaming like a disembodied existence?
- Are humans embodied minds? Or are we minded bodies?
- In Corinthians, Paul says that our natural bodies will be resurrected as 'spiritual bodies'. What could 'spiritual body' mean?

This question is not asking whether the mind can actually exist without the body, but whether that possibility is conceivable, whether it is conceptually coherent, or whether the idea is as nonsensical as dry rain. One way to approach the question would be to, after some discussion, run a thought experiment: who in the class can imagine a disembodied existence? Can they describe it? If there is a conflict of responses, you might then discuss why this is. Why can some people make sense of the idea while others cannot? Is it because the same words have different meanings for different people? Is it due to different experiences and different views of the world?

To further investigate the conceivability of a disembodied existence, you could set a writing task in which the class attempts to describe what such an existence would be like. This task is ludicrously vague and presupposes what it is trying to ascertain. To make it slightly less ludicrous you can frame it like this: 'Imagine you are made of snow. One spring morning you melt in the rising sun. You are now a puddle. Then, in the warmth of the day, you evaporate into the air. Describe what it would feel like to be an evaporated bodiless substance.'

Poetry can be better suited to such a task than prose, and the simpler the structure the better. Ask the class to begin each line with 'I feel …' and not to include rhyme, unless they want to. With the poems written you can then return to conceivability: do the poems show that a disembodied existence is actually conceivable? If so, does this show that our bodies are not essential to who we are?

Task Question 3   Are we our bodies?

Questions to take you further

- Is the mind the body?

- Is the mind part of the body?

- When you step on a nail, is the pain in your foot or your mind?

- When you are excited, is the excitement in your racing heart or your mind?

- Is thinking bodily?

- Is the body involved in everything we do?

- As the body changes, do we change with it? Can you imagine a child in an adult's body?

Conviction

Kant thought with his head and his spirit, but he never thought with his blood.

D. H. Lawrence

Imagine this speech being made in defence of a belief:

It is what I believe, an iron necessity. No matter what you teach me, the experiences I have, nothing will change my mind. Fire will freeze before I abandon my belief. It is who I am. I cannot betray my nature. This belief is a part of me. It is written in my bones. You can present me with evidence, tell me that doubt is a virtue, tell me it's good to question, that uncertainty is healthy, but where is your passion? Do you understand conviction? I cannot examine this belief beneath the cold gaze of light because this belief is the light itself. You want me to be level-headed, open, liberal. 'What if you are wrong?' you ask. 'You must be humble, accept the possibility of error.' The more reasonable you sound the less I can accept what you say. I will not change my mind because I cannot change it. It is not a question of choice, a matter of will, it is an object of belief.

Hermeneutic Question   What do you think the belief is?

Task Question 1   Is absolute belief good?

Questions to take you further

❖ Should we always be open to alternative points of view?

❖ Can we ever be certain of the truth?

❖ Is certainty a sign of madness?

❖ Can we deny our nature? Would it be wrong to try?

❖ Is belief a choice?

❖ Should we trust our own judgement above all else?

❖ Are there things experience cannot teach us?

Kierkegaard's *Fear and Trembling* is an attempt to come to terms with Abraham's willingness to follow God's command and sacrifice his beloved son, Isaac. Kierkegaard admires Abraham's faith, but he is also bewildered by it. In the midst of his bewilderment, he tells the story of a young man who is in love with a princess. The boy's love for her is vast, his whole life is founded on it, but the two cannot possibly be together (though Kierkegaard doesn't tell us why). His wishes are not realistic, reality has nullified them. Kierkegaard proposes three ways the prince may respond.

The first way of responding, Kierkegaard says, is characteristic of 'the frogs in life's swamp'. The frog will adapt to his circumstances and invest his heart in a more realistic love. He will get over it and move on.

The second way of responding belongs to the knight of infinite resignation. This knight will accept the world but refuse to renounce his love. He will resign himself to reality, but he will not temper his love. He will not forget the princess, but love her forever in a permanent state of loss, pining and forlorn, a life of sighs. Though the impossibility is accepted, he would rather live in pain than withdraw his heart.

The third way is the knight of faith's. Like the knight of infinite resignation, he will acknowledge the impossibility of his love whilst holding on to it, he will reconcile himself to the pain. But, unlike the knight of infinite resignation, he will still believe that he can be with the princess. He realises that it isn't merely unlikely, improbable or hard to imagine. He understands that it just *can't* happen. But he will both resign himself to the impossibility and continue to believe. He will say, 'It is impossible, that is why I believe it, because it is absurd. I will continue to hope though I know that my hope doesn't stand a chance. I will hope because it doesn't stand a chance.'

Task Question 2   Whose response is best: the frog's, the knight of infinite resignation's or the knight of faith's?

Questions to take you further

❖ Which of the three is the most defeated?

❖ Is it good to hope for the impossible?

❖ Is hope an unquestionable good?

❖ Can knowledge of the impossible coexist with belief in its possibility?

❖ Should we always adapt to reality? Should we always be prepared to change?

❖ Is change a form of self-betrayal?

❖ Are there impossibilities?

❖ Is it bad to give up?

❖ Are there always more fish in the sea?

In America, in the 19th century, a new kind of dawn was breaking upon philosophy. Beneath long skies, out of the raw land, the endless prairies, a philosophy known as pragmatism was announced. 'Pragmatic' derives from a Greek word for action, and action is at the heart of pragmatism. Pragmatism is concerned with the practical difference our beliefs make; it is focused on the consequences of our beliefs, the fruits they deliver, their effectiveness, utility and helpfulness. Pragmatists claim that truth is an instrument to living and that usefulness confers truth; they would justify a given belief by saying, 'It is true because it is useful.' Writing in 1907, these words are taken from William James:

[For pragmatism the] only test of probable truth is what works best in the way of leading us, what fits every part of life best … if the notion of God, in particular, should prove to do it, how should pragmatism deny God's existence? She could see no meaning in treating as 'not true' a notion that was pragmatically so successful … Truth is *made*.

[When evaluating whether a belief is true pragmatism asks] 'what concrete difference will its being true make in anyone's actual life? … What, in short, is the truth's cash-value in experiential terms?' … an idea is 'true' so long as to believe it is profitable to our lives … *The true is the name of whatever proves itself to be good in the way of belief.*

Task Question 3 Do you agree with James' ideas? Does the usefulness of a belief make it true?

Questions to take you further

- Why do we call things 'true'?
- Can a useless belief be true?
- Is truth a human affair? Is the world a human affair?
- Should we always believe in what is useful to us?
- Would it be wrong to try and make a person abandon a useful belief?
- Are there more important things than usefulness?
- Is truth different for different people?
- Can truth be bad for us?

Emotion

and kisses are a better fate
than wisdom

E. E. Cummings

Our common behaviour is ordinary-strange.

- ❖ We scream when we are frightened.
- ❖ We shout when we are angry.
- ❖ We cry when we are sad.
- ❖ We laugh when we are happy.
- ❖ We tut when we are annoyed.

Starter Question 1 Why *do* we do these things?

Questions to take you further

- ❖ Is this behaviour irrational?
- ❖ Does this behaviour have a purpose?
- ❖ Is this behaviour arbitrary?
- ❖ Why are there patterns of behaviour? When we are sad, why don't we laugh just as often as we cry?

You might just want to focus on one of these, or all of them, or an example of your own.

According to the Book of Genesis, sibling rivalry started at the beginning, with the first siblings, the brothers Cain and Abel:

Adam made love to his wife Eve, and she became pregnant and gave birth to Cain. She said, 'With the help of the Lord I have brought forth a man.' Later she gave birth to his brother Abel.

Now Abel kept flocks, and Cain worked the soil. In the course of time Cain brought some of the fruits of the soil as an offering to the Lord. And Abel also brought an offering – fat portions from some of the firstborn of his flock. The Lord looked with favor on Abel and his offering, but on Cain and his offering he did not look with favor. So Cain was very angry, and his face was downcast.

Then the Lord said to Cain, 'Why are you angry? Why is your face downcast? If you do what is right, will you not be accepted? But if you do not do what is right, sin is crouching at your door; it desires to have you, but you must rule over it.'

Now Cain said to his brother Abel, 'Let's go out to the field.' While they were in the field, Cain attacked his brother Abel and killed him.

Then the Lord said to Cain, 'Where is your brother Abel?'

'I don't know,' he replied. 'Am I my brother's keeper?'

The Lord said, 'What have you done? Listen! Your brother's blood cries out to me from the ground. Now you are under a curse and driven from the ground, which opened its mouth to receive your brother's blood from your hand. When you work the ground, it will no longer yield its crops for you. You will be a restless wanderer on the earth.'

To illustrate the story you could show Titian's Cain and Abel.

Hermeneutic Question   Why did Cain kill Abel?

Questions to take you further

- Was he trying to achieve something?
- Did he want revenge?
- What is revenge and why do we want it?
- Did he have alternatives?
- What would Cain have said when God asked him, 'Why are you angry?'

Starter Question 2   What is anger?

Questions to take you further

- What does it feel like? How does it change us?
- Does it have a point?
- What is it a response to?
- What satisfies it? What does it want?
- What does it hate?
- What would have to change about our nature to stop us experiencing it?

Task Question 1   Should we have been made without anger?

Questions to take you further

- Without anger, would Cain have killed Abel?
- Without anger, would anyone hurt anyone?
- Do some people deserve or need to be hurt?
- Do we need anger?

Two thousand years ago, the Roman philosopher Seneca wrote an essay on anger addressed to his brother. Seneca was a Stoic (though, ironically, he taught the violent and wrathful emperor Nero and died by suicide at Nero's command). Stoicism believes in the value of serenity, in never getting worked up or carried away. It is against emotion.

Seneca described anger as 'a departure from sanity'. He said, 'No emotion has a more turbulent look. It mars the loveliest face, turns the calmest countenance into something grim … The veins swell. The breast heaves with rapid panting; the voice bursts out in fury and the neck strains. Then the limbs tremble, the hands cannot keep still, the whole body tosses. What can the mind be within, do you think, if the outward image is so foul? … anger in itself is hideous.'

In his essay, Seneca responds to several points made in favour of anger.

You could present the following passage by first asking the class how they would respond if they were arguing against the points made in anger's favour, and then looking at Seneca's responses.

But against enemies there is need for anger. Nowhere less. The requirement there is not for impulses to be poured out, but to remain well tuned and responsive. Gladiators are protected by skill but left defenceless by anger. What is the need for anger when reason serves as well? Do you suppose the hunter to be angry with the prey? He catches it as it comes, pursues it as it flees – and all this is done, without anger, by reason.

Is the good man not angry if he sees his father slain and his mother ravished? No, he will not be angry. He will punish and protect. Why should not filial devotion, even without anger, be enough of a stimulus? You could argue in the same way: 'Tell me then, if he sees his father or son undergoing surgery, will the good man not weep or faint?' The good man will do his duty, undismayed and undaunted.

Good men are angry at wrongs done to their friends. Anger for one's friends is the mark of a weak mind, not a devoted one. What is fine and honourable is to go forth in defence of parents, children, friends and fellow-citizens, under the guidance of duty itself, in the exercise of the will – not through some ravaging impulse. No affection is keener to punish than anger is. For that very reason, it is ill fitted for punishing. Headlong and mindless like almost every burning desire, it gets in the way of what it rushes to do.

Anger is of use because it makes men keener to fight. On that principle, drunkenness would be useful – it makes men reckless and bold. Aristotle says that some emotions, if well used, serve as arms. That would be true if, like weapons of war, they could be picked up and put down at will. But these arms which Aristotle would give to virtue go to war by themselves, without awaiting the hand of the warrior. They possess us; they are not our possessions.

But there is pleasure in anger – paying back pain is sweet. Not in the slightest! He who pays back pain with pain is doing wrong. Instead of moderating our anger, we should eliminate it altogether – for how can there be moderation of a thing that is bad?

Task Question 2   Is anger good?

Questions to take you further

* Is anger helpful?
* Is it a good moral motivation? Is it a necessary moral motivation?
* Is it a departure from sanity?
* Is it heartless?

- Can anger be kind? Is it incompatible with kindness?

- Is it natural?

- Plato wrote, 'A good man does no damage.' Do you agree?

The Stoics also argued for the elimination of fear, which, like anger, is another source of irrationality. Their view of fear persists today in what we call 'phobias'. Phobias are idiosyncratic fears. Whereas all sane people would be scared of a lion, the fear of, say, buttons, is somewhat more particular and personal.

Phobias are democratic, affecting the courageous and cowardly alike; even Julius Caesar hid in terror at the sound of thunder. Psychiatry manuals tell us that phobias are fears that are 'excessive or unreasonable'. One of our most common idiosyncratic fears is the fear of spiders: arachnophobia.

The fear of spiders is present in nursery rhymes ('Little Miss Muffet') and urban legends (tales of exploding cacti and toilet-seat bites). In areas of southern Italy, it is believed that if you are bitten by a spider you will become possessed by it and die. The only remedy is to perform the tarantism ritual, which involves dancing for several days in a bid to expel the spider's poison. No scientific basis to either the illness or the cure has been found.

Task Question 3   Is there such a thing as an irrational fear?

Questions to take you further

- Is there such a thing as a rational fear?

- Is arachnophobia rational?

- Is fear bad?

- Are there things we should be afraid of?

- ❖ Is fear necessary to avoid danger? Is fear helpful in avoiding danger?

- ❖ Is danger subjective? Are we all vulnerable in different ways?

- ❖ Is there such a thing as an overreaction?

- ❖ What is fear?

Desire

Praise God for this desire,
and let it intensify!

Hafiz

Starter Question 1   What is desire?

Questions to take you further

- ❖ How would the world be different if there were no desires?

- ❖ Why do humans desire? Where does it come from?

- ❖ Is it a force or a lack or something else?

- ❖ What is the difference between a want and a need?

- ❖ Do we start desiring from birth or is it something we grow into?

- ❖ Why do our desires change?

In the 19th century, the German composer Richard Wagner adapted a medieval love story into an opera called *Tristan und Isolde*. The story tells of a princess and a knight who are overcome with passion for each other after they mistakenly drink a love potion. But their love is a living impossibility: she is betrothed to marry his king. Ultimately they die for their desire.

The opera opens on a ship. The princess, Isolde, has been forcefully taken from her native Ireland to marry the king of Cornwall, King Marke. The knight, Tristan, is the orchestrator. He suggested the marriage to King Marke and he is captaining the mission to collect the bride.

Isolde is distraught and wishes the winds would rise up and sink the ship. Her rage is particularly focused on Tristan – the pair already know each other. Isolde recounts how they met, how she had once found a wounded man drifting in a boat off the Irish coast. She healed him and restored his health, but she came to realise that the splinter in the body of her dead fiancé corresponded to the wood of the foreigner's sword. This man, who had told her his name was Tantris, was in fact Tristan, the murderer of her future husband.

As Tristan slept, Isolde held his sword over the bed ready to kill him, but at that moment he awoke and their eyes locked. His gaze disarmed her and she released the sword. Without revealing his identity to her countrymen, she let him sail safely back to Cornwall.

But in return for her clemency, Tristan has pried her from her home and ensnared her in a marriage she has no interest in. She feels betrayed and, for a second time, she wishes to kill him. Tristan accepts her wish. However, the death potion Isolde asks for is switched with a love potion by her maid. Both Tristan and Isolde drink from the bottle, both thinking they will die. As they look into each other's eyes they feel a surge of love and death does not come. They fall into each other's arms, love-locked and assailed with longing. The voice of the sailors announces their arrival at Cornwall.

The maid regrets what she has done, foreseeing the fatality of the love, but Isolde reassures her that she did nothing; it is the work of Frau Minne, the divine personification of love. Possessed of this illicit love, Tristan and Isolde are only able to meet in the secrecy of night. They come to identify their love of each other with a love of night and a longing for death. Their love is forbidden by day, the watched world of duty, and only death offers the promise of lasting union. 'So let us die and never part,' Isolde sings.

One moonlit summer night, as the two are drawing closer to one another amid a veil of trees, their privacy is abruptly ended by the entrance of the king. He is heartbroken and dismayed to discover Tristan's betrayal. Melot, the man who led the king to the garden, challenges Tristan. Tristan lunges forward but withdraws his weapon, allowing Melot's sword to enter his body, and he collapses.

The final act opens with Tristan at his home castle dying and delirious with longing. Only Isolde, with her ability to heal, can save him. As the arrival of her ship is announced, Tristan tears off his bandages so that he may die in her arms, so that his wounds may be healed with eternity. He speaks her name as she cradles him to death and they exchange a final look. King Marke enters to find Isolde holding the cooling body. The king grieves for Tristan, explaining that he had learnt of the potion and had come to offer his forgiveness and unite the pair. But Isolde is oblivious; she has begun her journey from life.

Taken by the cloud of Tristan's spirit, she feels his presence in waves and sounds and fragrances; she fades into his unearthly existence and happily dies, the 'highest bliss'.

The story needs the music (and libretto), so this outline should be accompanied by clips from the opera – there are subtitled productions available on YouTube. Moments to show: the taking and effect of the potion, the garden interruption, King Marke's dismay and the final aria, 'Liebestod'.

If the class is not familiar with opera, before you start on desire, it would be nice to discuss their first impressions of this novel art form, the question simply being: what do you think of opera? (Here I'm thinking of Barthes: 'If I agree to judge a text according to pleasure, I cannot go on to say: this one is good, that bad. The text can wring from me only this judgement, in no way adjectival: that's it!') To lead into the Hermeneutic Question, you might ask whether they think opera is a good medium for a love story, and what they think of the opera's portrayal of love. Is this what love is like? Is this what love ought to be like?

Pupils may find Wagner boring, and you can invite this response. If you think boredom might make for an interesting discussion, below are a set of questions that provide the session with an alternative path, one that avoids the Hermeneutic Question. The paths rejoin at Buddhism. You can get underway with boredom by asking the Wagner sceptics, 'Many people think this opera is a masterpiece, but you find it boring. Is there something wrong with you or the opera?' and then pursue the following:

Starter Question 2   What is boredom?

Questions to take you further

❖ What causes it?

❖ What cures it?

❖ What does it feel like? Does it feel like anything? Can it be described?

❖ Is there anything that can be done to permanently avoid it?

❖ Can you be bored without knowing it?

❖ What is the relation between boredom and desire?

A parent knocks on her daughter's door and finds her still in bed.

'You will be late for school,' the parent says.

'I'm not going to school.'

'Are you ill?'

'No, I feel fine,' the daughter says.

'So why aren't you going?'

'Because it's boring.'

Task Question (1)   Is boredom a good reason not to go to school?

Questions to take you further

❖ Is boredom a problem with us or the world?

❖ Should we do things even if they bore us?

❖ Is desire, and the prospect of pleasure, the only good reason to do anything?

❖ Are there things we should do out of duty? Is boredom irrelevant?

❖ Are you responsible for your boredom?

'What are you going to do with your day, then?' the parent says.

'Nothing.'

'Why not go shopping?'

'That's boring.'

'Cinema?'

'Boring.'

'You could go to the beach.'

'Boring.'

'You can't just do nothing.'

'What can I do? Everything is boring.'

Task Question (2)   If a person found nothing in the world interesting, would this be a kind of illness?

Questions to take you further

❖ Would it be a kind of blindness?

❖ Is the world intrinsically interesting?

❖ Is it unnatural to have no desires?

❖ Is there anything wrong with doing nothing?

❖ By what criteria should we classify a mental state as an illness?

Task Question (3)   Is boredom bad?

Questions to take you further

❖ Is it laziness?

❖ Is it ignorance?

❖ Is it spoilt, ungrateful? Should we always be grateful and content with what we have?

❖ Is it a lack of imagination?

❖ Is boredom rude? Is it better to hide our boredom rather than offend others?

❖ Why do we dislike having nothing to do? Horses seem fine with it.

❖ Why isn't boredom an experience we seek out?

❖ If you could remove from humans the capacity to feel bored, would you?

❖ Kierkegaard wrote, 'Boredom is the root of all evil.' What do you think this means?

If you've taken the boredom path, skip the following Hermeneutic Question and continue on with Task Question 1. Buddhism and its attempt to exorcise desire can be read as a solution to boredom. If we never desired desire, if desire were not something we wanted, waited or hoped for, perhaps, then, we would never be bored.

Hermeneutic Question   Did Tristan and Isolde really love each other?

Questions to take you further

- Is there such a thing as fake love and fake desire?
- Are some of our wants more real than others?
- Do we want everything we want?
- Are we responsible for our desires?
- Do we choose our desires or are they like spells we fall under?
- Is their wish to die together an expression of love? Is love suicidal?
- Should King Marke have forgiven Tristan?

This question can be taken a couple of ways. On the one hand, there's the question, which the bullet points are centred on, of whether the role of the potion means their love is somehow artificial; on the other hand, there's the question of whether the necrophilic aspect of their feelings offers a good picture of what love is.

Like Wagner's Tristan and Isolde, the Buddha saw desire as a problem, a source of suffering, and they all agreed that sacrifice was the solution. For Tristan and Isolde, desire is only satisfied in sacrifice, in death. For the Buddha, however, it is desire that should be sacrificed, not life. Whereas Tristan and Isolde believed you must die for your desire, the Buddha believed it was desire that must die for the good of your life.

The Buddha saw the world as 'always burning with desire'.

All the world is on fire,
All the world is burning,
All the world is ablaze,
All the world is quaking.

His fundamental pursuit was the cessation of suffering. He believed that desire was the cause of all misery, suffering and discontent.

Whatever suffering arose in the past, all that arose rooted in desire, with desire as its source; for desire is the root of suffering. Whatever suffering will arise in the future, all that will arise rooted in desire, with desire as its source; for desire is the root of suffering.

Without desire there would be no suffering. Life would be better. To escape suffering the Buddha attempted to empty himself of all desire, and he believed he was successful:

I am desireless, unattached, disengaged;
My vision of all things has been purified.

Task Question 1   Is it possible not to desire?

Questions to take you further

❖ Is desire bad for us?

- Is it possible to have too much desire? Is it possible to have too little?

- Is desire essential to life?

- Is desire inevitably tragic? Is it a form of suffering? Is frustration suffering?

- Is the end of desire the end of suffering?

- Is the world 'always burning with desire'? Is fire an appropriate metaphor for desire?

- Are we ever satisfied?

- Are you more sympathetic to Wagner's view or the Buddha's?

- Can we end suffering?

The Buddha conceived of the cessation of desire as emancipation. He believed that desire binds us like 'birds caught in a snare':

By desire is the world bound;
By the removal of desire it is freed.
Desire is what one must forsake
To cut off all bondage.

Imagine you love chocolate cake. Whenever you see a slice you can't help but feel hungry, you can't help wanting a bite.

Task Question 2   Does loving chocolate cake mean that you are not free?

Questions to take you further

- Do we have control over the things we want?

- Do the things we want have control over us?
- Do we choose our desires? Is choice necessary for freedom?
- Is desire addiction?
- Would you rather have freedom or desire?
- What is freedom for? Why is it good?

Society

'We'

Every strong soul must put off its connection with this society, its vanity and chiefly its fear.

D. H. Lawrence

Perfectibility

To your faults be true.

W. H. Auden

According to Greek myth, Prometheus stole fire from the gods and gave it to mortals. It is thought that this gift strengthened our minds. It gave us the power to progress and flourish, to improve ourselves and become better.

For his theft Prometheus was severely punished. Zeus, the god of all gods, chained him to a rock and left him to the mercy of nature.

As Prometheus lay locked beneath the sun an eagle circled overhead. Realising that Prometheus could not escape, the eagle swooped down and landed on his torso, piercing the skin with its claws. It looked Prometheus over, biding its time, relishing the helplessness of its prey. With vacant eyes it hooked its beak into Prometheus' flesh and ate his liver, one piece at a time.

That night Prometheus' liver grew back and the next morning the eagle returned. Once again, through screaming and tears, it methodically consumed Prometheus' liver. This pattern repeated itself for the next 30,000 years.

Imagine you had the gall to steal powers from the gods.

Starter Question Would you use the power of a god to change anything about human beings?

As well as asking the pupils what they would change, ask them how they would do this. For example, if someone says they would make humans more consider-ate of the environment, ask them what they would need to change about human nature to accomplish this (such changes will generally involve adding or taking something away, for example, adding sympathy, taking greed).

Task Question 1 Are human beings a disappointment?

Questions to take you further

❖ Are human beings flawed?

❖ Should we be better than we actually are?

❖ Can we be better than we actually are?

❖ Are we good enough?

❖ Are some people more/less flawed than others?

❖ If we are flawed, were we made this way?

❖ What can we compare ourselves to in order to know whether we are flawed or not?

❖ Is everyone doing the best they can?

❖ If we aren't flawed, does that mean we are perfect?

You can use the ideas taken from the Starter Question as the context to this question. If there were proposed changes to humanity, does this imply that humanity leaves much to be desired, that humanity is lacking in certain respects, that humanity is flawed? If it ain't broke, why fix it?

In 1920s Russia, a group of revolutionaries called the Bolsheviks believed that Prometheus could be more than a myth. They believed they could change the world, and in so doing, change humans too. It was thought that, like technology (our modern-day fire), humans could be engineered to become better, to progress. Leon Trotsky, a Bolshevik leader, wrote:

> The human species will enter into a state of radical transformation. Man will become immeasurably stronger, wiser and subtler; his body will become more harmonised, his movements more rhythmic, his voice more musical. The average human type will rise to the heights of an Aristotle, a Goethe, or a Marx. And above this ridge new peaks will rise.

These were not idle fantasies. During the 1920s, the Russians tried to create what they believed would be a perfect form of human by attempting to cross-breed humans with chimpanzees. They believed that human perfection was possible, but their experiments failed.

Task Question 2   Could there be a perfect human?

Questions to take you further

❖ Can you imagine a perfect human? What would s/he be like?

❖ Do humans progress?

❖ What is progress?

❖ Are some people more perfect than others?

❖ Is there a limit to how good a person can be? Who has come closest to that limit?

❖ Can humans improve infinitely? Is there an end point?

❖ Are we essentially flawed? Is perfection beyond us?

❖ What is perfection? What is its opposite?

- If you wouldn't change anything about something, does that mean it is perfect?

- Is there something flawed about the idea of perfection? Is the idea anti-human?

This last Task Question can wander in a number of directions; for example, it might lead into a discussion on pluralism and whether the idea of perfection renounces the variety of people and things in the world. It might lead into theology and the question of whether Christ was human. It could, moreover, lead into a discussion on the models of female perfection – plastic surgery, weight control, chastity – that exist in the culture and the misogynistic basis of these. Whether the culture harbours prescriptive notions of male perfection might also be questioned.

Focusing on the final bullet point, and the idea of perfection generally, you could ask the class whether they can think of perfect instances of anything. If you cannot conceive of a perfect person, or at least don't believe that such perfection is possible, can you conceive of, or have you encountered, say, a perfect meal? Or a perfect sound? Or smell? Or sentence? Or painting? Or flower? Or weather? Is perfection, of any kind, real?

Utopia

I would never want to belong to a club that would have someone like me for a member.

Woody Allen

This is a cousin of the previous session. Rather than focusing on the perfectibility of the individual, it considers the perfectibility of society.

A utopia is a perfect society that exists nowhere. Indeed, *nowhere* is what the word means. Utopias are imaginary places, plans for a new beginning, designed to show us how good things could be if only we would listen.

Many writers have described utopias, including Plato, who believed an ideal society would have no families; Francis Bacon, who thought that science could civilise us; John Milton, who believed our paradisiacal lives, in which we were shamelessly naked and ate fruit and frolicked with lions, were ruined by sin; William Morris, who wanted punishment and school to be abolished, and embroidery embraced; and H. G. Wells, who advocated the sterilisation of 'unfit' people.

In 1915 D. H. Lawrence went a step further and seriously considered enacting his moneyless utopia – 'Every strong soul must put off its connection with this society, its vanity and chiefly its fear' – wondering which of his friends he should invite along to the island he would call Rananim.

By showing us our potential perfection, utopias expose our real degradation; by telling us how wonderful society might be, they are telling us how bad it actually is. A utopia is dismay cloaked in desire.

Utopias are rebirths. By making a new society built on fresh foundations, they teach us how we can revolutionise the quality of our lives together. Utopias are characterised by a pervasive and embedded sense of harmony, order and purpose, which is often achieved through technology, freedom or reason.

The following utopias borrow some common themes and ideas:

1. This society refers to itself as the Great Family. Its people call their elders mother or father and their equals brother or sister. The leader is not 'prime minister' or 'president', but the Supreme Father or the Supreme Mother. The motto of the society is: One people, One blood. Every morning at 0900 workers and schoolchildren recite The Pledge: 'I belong to the Great Family.'

I am a child of the Supreme Father. I will strive to honour the Family and the Father. I will never turn away. Security, Permanence, Loyalty – these are our founding principles and I will give all that I am to preserve them.' In this society there is no marriage because the Great Family is the only family. Adults are randomly selected to reproduce and rear, and this task is performed out of civic duty rather than personal affection.

Conscription is in force. Between the ages of 14 and 18 all people serve in the armed forces. It is believed that this helps to shape proud and courageous citizens. At 18 they begin working in the job that was assigned to them at birth, and which they will have till death. Children are trained to only perform these jobs; they are not educated in irrelevant subjects. Only children whose future careers require literacy are taught to read and write. The government is responsible for producing all books and films, which contain instructive messages about unity and fidelity. There are no elections and the leader is not voted for; as they all say, family is not a matter of choice, but destiny. There is no poverty or unemployment. Crime is negligible. Government happiness surveys show that 98% of the population report feeling, 'suitably positive about life'.

2. It may not be right to call this collection of people a society. They live in a vast area of wilderness, though they do not live together. They lead solitary and self-sufficient lives. Though there is some trade, people mostly fend for themselves. They grow their own food, build their own homes and make their own clothes. Contact with others is rare, and if it occurs, it can be brutal. There are no laws binding these people together. Everything is regarded as a private affair. If someone is killed and their property stolen, it is the responsibility of the family to seek retribution, if they so wish. People are not wantonly aggressive towards one another, but they are defensive of their territory, and they are determined survivors. If their crop has failed, they will

see nothing wrong in taking from others. There is no sense of morality, no belief in how things ought to be, only the acceptance that power and strength are the determinants of how things are.

3. This society has no crime, no mental disorders; there are no physical disabilities and no terminal illnesses. The average life expectancy is 105. It is a technologically sophisticated society that achieves its successes through its ability to manipulate and decide the genetic make-up of its citizens. No child is born 'naturally'. It is law that every conception undergoes genetic screening and there are certain traits that geneticists are legally obliged to remove; for example, it is a criminal offence to allow the Alzheimer's gene to pass through screening.

In this society the idea of curing a disease is seen as a medical relic, not too dissimilar from the way we think of bleeding patients today. Diseases do not need to be cured because they are prevented from existing in the first place. Cancer is non-existent. Moreover, genes that entail a predisposition towards crime have been discovered and the law requires these to be screened out. This also applies to genes responsible for depression, bipolar disorder, 'subversive tendency disorder' (a classification not known to us but described as 'an inclination towards anti-authority attitudes and behaviour', which, it is claimed, 'is not bad in itself, but results in other mental health issues brought about by excessive levels of stress and frustration') and other such mental illnesses.

Despite these laws the society regards itself as tolerant and pluralistic. Parents are offered a great deal of choice. For example, they are free to decide the sex, and sexuality, of their children. They are also free to leave these things to chance, though many parents do not. Most choose to select the personalities and appearance of their children. For example, they may wish to give their child the eventual physique of an athlete, the IQ of a chess champion or the imagination of an artist. Despite the declared pluralism of the society, there are, of course, fashion trends. Just as in our society there may be decades where the name Britney is popular, so too in this society there are decades in which many babies grow to physically resemble particular actors or singers. But fashion is an expression of freedom and this society believes that its gene-technology enables and extends our ability to live as free individuals.

Starter Question 1   Which utopia is the best? Which utopia is the worst?

Questions to take you further

❖ Which utopia is the most/least realistic?

❖ What do you think each utopia feels is wrong with our present society?

❖ Do any of the utopias share similarities with our own society?

Starter Question 2   What would your utopia be like?

This question can be approached as a group brainstorming session in which you compile the class's miscellaneous proposals. Or you might want to split the class into smaller groups, asking each one to collaborate, negotiate and write down the fundamentals of their shared utopia, producing a manifesto of sorts. This exercise can be extended further; for example, you could select two groups whose utopias are significantly different and ask them to compete in convincing the class that their Nowhere is the best Nowhere. You could then have the class take an anonymous vote (anonymity adds to the suspense) in order to decide which utopia the class should embark upon together.

The campaign/debate can be loosely structured round the British parliamentary style. Speakers from each group alternate, with each new speaker introducing and explaining an additional feature of their utopia, or giving an elaboration of a previous feature, and offering a critique of the ideas of their opposite number. Every speaker has an equal and limited time – a minute works well – with the final speaker having the job of summarising the brilliance of their group's utopia and the inadequacies of the opposition's. If you want to more actively involve the rest of the class, you could allow them to offer points of information, i.e. interjectory questions or comments that challenge the argument of the speaker.

Task Question 1 Is our society drastically flawed?

Questions to take you further

❖ What are the best things about our society?

❖ What are the worst things about our society?

❖ Who is responsible for its flaws?

Task Question 2 Could there be a perfect society?

Questions to take you further

❖ Is there a limit to how good a society can be?

❖ How close is our society to that limit?

❖ Can we improve infinitely? Is there an end point?

❖ Are we essentially flawed? Is perfection beyond us?

❖ Is there something flawed in the idea of perfection?

Property

O curse of marriage,
That we can call these delicate creatures ours
And not their appetites!

Othello

Starter Question   Think of something you own. What does 'I own this' mean?

There are at least two parts to this question: what makes you the owner? And what are the entitlements of ownership? With the first, if it is said that something is owned when it has been bought, you can follow this up by asking what made the person it was bought from the owner, and proceed far enough into the object's history to reach the point at which money wasn't involved – to this end you could ask: in a world without money would anyone own anything? You might also ask whether money correlates to a social convention or enshrines an exchange of objective right, i.e. is it yours morally or conventionally? In other words, what makes theft wrong?

We tend to say of the things we own they are 'mine'. Pursuing this, ask the class to think of those things they would prefix with 'my', for example, 'My toes', 'My school', 'My birthday', 'My God'. Does the 'my' prefix always mean ownership? If not, what else does it mean? Can a thing be ours without being owned by us?

Slavery has always existed. The Egyptians kept slaves. The Romans and Greeks kept slaves (the Romans captured slaves from Britain). Before the introduction of the Atlantic slave trade, slavery was already practised throughout Africa.

The Atlantic slave trade was orchestrated by European countries. Over the course of 350 years, 12 million Africans were kidnapped from their homes and shipped in chains across the Atlantic Ocean to work and die as slaves. Many worked on sugar plantations, labouring to satisfy the sweet tooth of Europeans.

In 1807 Britain made slave trading illegal and 58 years later America abolished slavery altogether. Slavery, however, still exists in the world today.

What is a slave? A slave is a person who has been captured, sold and forced to work. In 1768, for example, a 24-year-old man could be bought for around £90 to work as a coal miner. The slave has no say in what happens to them; a slave is a person who is treated as if they were a machine. It is as if we could enter a shop with the option of buying either a washing machine or a washing slave. Once you have bought the slave, they are your property. You are said to own them, you are their master (though we might wonder why we don't speak of ourselves as the masters of our washing machines).

This is a description from a traveller who visited the tobacco plantations in Virginia, America:

The Negroes are very numerous, some gentlemen having hundreds of them of all sorts, to whom they bring great profit; for the sake of which they are obliged to keep them well, and not overwork, starve, or famish them. Though indeed some masters, careless of their own interest and reputation, are too cruel and negligent.

This account views slaves as engines of profit. In the 6th century, however, an African poet, Suhaym, who was born into slavery, believed that he was far more than his status. He wrote: 'Though I am a slave my soul is nobly free.'

Hermeneutic Question 1   What do you think Suhaym meant by this?

Task Question 1   Is it possible to own people?

Questions to take you further

❖ Is it possible to own a person's soul/mind?

❖ Is it possible to own a person's body?

❖ Can a person be both free and owned?

❖ Can we be controlled by others?

❖ Are we, in any sense, the product of other people?

❖ What does it mean to be someone's master?

❖ Does being responsible for a person make you the owner of them?

❖ Is it possible to own anything in nature?

Here you can apply the answers given in the Starter Question; for example, if it was said that being a thing's maker makes you its owner, you can ask whether people are made – if so, by whom – and whether their makers are their owners. And if it was said that owning something means being able to treat it in any way you please, does this also apply to owned people? For example, if parents own their children because they 'made' them, does this mean they are free to treat their children however they please, just as they could scratch their own car if they felt like it.

The following Hermeneutic Questions are a prelude to a consideration of self-ownership. Whereas God's answer to Moses speaks of the self as a whole and simple thing, Iago's self is fragmentary and divided. Whether we are together or in pieces may be significant to the question of whether we own ourselves. Can we own something elusive and conflicted?

In Exodus we are told that God appeared to Moses in a burning bush. At this time the Israelites were being held as slaves in Egypt. God said to Moses that he would help the Israelites escape their persecution and that it would be Moses who would lead them.

Moses, wondering how he could describe this encounter to the Israelites, asked God his name. God said, 'I am that I am.'

Hermeneutic Question 2   What do you think God meant by this?

Question to take you further

❖   Could God's answer be true of us?

The events of Shakespeare's play *Othello* are governed by a wicked and mischievous character named Iago. Using lies and intelligence, Iago plots to ruin Othello's young marriage, convincing Othello of his wife's infidelity. Undone by jealousy and despair, Othello murders his wife only to discover that she was innocent and unwavering in her devotion. He then takes his own life. Iago's plan is a success.

Who was Iago? Why was he so cruel? Early in the play he inverts God's words and says, 'I am not what I am.'

Hermeneutic Question 3   What do you think Iago meant by this?

Question to take you further

❖   Could Iago's answer be true of us?

Task Question 2   Do we own ourselves?

Questions to take you further

❖ Do we own our souls/minds? Do we own our bodies?

❖ Do we own our desires?

❖ Do we own our lives?

❖ Can we lose ownership of ourselves?

❖ Do your parents own you?

❖ Are we unowned or just unownable?

❖ Do we have power over ourselves?

❖ Are we our own makers?

❖ Are we responsible for ourselves?

❖ What is the opposite of being owned?

❖ What are we?

One way to approach this question would be to first ask for a list of possible answers to the question: who owns you? (e.g. no one, nature, parents, yourself, government, teachers, time, desires, conscience, God) Then, during an extended talk time, ask the class to write these down and order them from 1 to n: from that which has the most claim over us to that which has the least. After discussing their various orderings, you can focus the discussion specifically on the Task Question.

Task Question 3   Is everything in the world owned by someone?

Questions to take you further

❖ Is there anything that is, or ought to be, owned by everyone?

❖ Is there anything it is impossible to lose ownership of?

❖ If God exists, does He own everything?

Intelligence

There is nothing in our book, the Qur'an, that teaches us to suffer peacefully. Our religion teaches us to be intelligent.

Malcolm X

Starter Question 1   Who are the most intelligent people you can think of? What about them is intelligent?

Starter Question 2   What is intelligence?

As a follow-up consider asking: 'How does intelligence help us? What is it good for?' A pragmatic spin anchors a question back to everyday life and can be useful in making a question/topic feel more tangible.

IQ is an acronym for Intelligence Quotient; it is a measure of how much intelligence you have. This is an example of the kind of question you'd be asked in an IQ test:

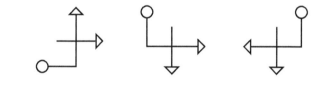

a.

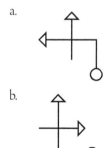

b.

c.

d.

Hermeneutic Question 1   Which figure is next in the series?

Question to take you further

❖ If you can't figure it out, does that mean you are unintelligent?

Task Question 1   Can intelligence be measured?

Questions to take you further

❖ Can the intelligence between people be compared?

❖ Are some people more intelligent than others?

❖ Does intelligence mean something different to everyone? Is it a matter of style?

❖ Who should decide how intelligence is measured? (If the most intelligent people should decide, how would we know who they were if there wasn't already a measure for intelligence?)

❖ Should intelligence be measured?

❖ Which of our features and attributes can't be measured?

The Ancient Greek philosopher Plato suggested that intelligence is like a light that allows us to see what other people can't. Those who lack intelligence are those who are blind, in darkness, unable to truly understand the world. The dialogue below, written by Plato, considers the political significance of intelligence:

'If a guard is keeping an eye on something, is it obvious whether he should be blind or have good eyesight?'

'Of course it's obvious.'

'Can you see a difference between those who are blind and those who are genuinely lacking in knowledge of everything that is? They can't look at what is most real, and in this way establish rules about beauty, justice and goodness in everyday life.'

'No, I can't,' he said. 'There is no difference to speak of between these people and the blind.'

'Are these the people we shall appoint as rulers, then? Or the ones who do know about each thing that is, who are the equal of the others in experience of practical affairs, and not inferior in any other area of human excellence?'

'If they are equal in other matters, then it would be absurd not to choose this second group, since on grounds of knowledge – which is the single most important thing – they come out on top.'

Hermeneutic Question 2   What is being argued for in this passage?

In short, just as you would want the driver of a car to be the person with the best eyesight, Plato suggested those who possess control of society, those with the most power, should be those who are the most intelligent.

This sentiment was echoed hundreds of years later by the philosopher Thomas Aquinas: 'Men of outstanding intelligence naturally take command, while those who are less intelligent … seem intended by nature to act as servants.'

Task Question 2   Should the most intelligent people have the most power?

Questions to take you further

* Is intelligence like sight? Does intelligence mean being able to see the world clearer than other people?
* Is intelligence a talent that people are born with?
* Do some people understand the world better than others?
* Is knowledge the 'single most important thing' for a ruler?
* How should it be decided who has power?
* Should anyone have more power than anyone else?

When asking pupils the reasons for their views, bring them back to the dialogue and ask them to identify moments in the passage that they either consent or object to.

Task Question 3   Do we need intelligence?

Questions to take you further

* Do we need intelligence to survive?
* Do we need intelligence to live well?
* Do we need intelligence to be good people?
* Do babies need intelligence?
* Do animals need intelligence?
* Do trees need intelligence?
* Is intelligence a good thing?

Morality and the Law

One Law for the Lion and Ox is Oppression.

William Blake

Starter Question 1   What is the law?

Questions to take you further

- ❖ What is it for?
- ❖ Who makes it? In a democracy, is it effectively made by the people?
- ❖ Why do we speak of 'breaking' the law?
- ❖ Is morality distinct from the law?
- ❖ Why do we have the laws we do?

Starter Question 2   Are there laws you disagree with?

Questions to take you further

- ❖ Should we follow laws we disagree with?
- ❖ Can breaking a law be a way of changing it?
- ❖ Can changing a law be a way of breaking it?

You might like to raise examples, such as drug laws, or the Police Reform and Social Responsibility Act 2011 which prohibits freely camping or protesting in Parliament Square, or the Immigration Act 1971 which allows immigrants to be detained indefinitely.

Crime and Punishment is a novel by the Russian writer Fyodor Dostoyevsky, which tells the story of a young man, Raskolnikov, who murders two women in an attempt to prove that he is extraordinary, special, a man above the law.

This is a summary of his ideas:

All men are divided into 'ordinary' and 'extraordinary'. Ordinary men have to live in submission, have no right to transgress the law, because, don't you see, they are ordinary. But extraordinary men have a right to commit any crime and to transgress the law in any way, just because they are extraordinary.

After he has committed the murders, he confesses the crime to a friend:

'I wanted to murder without casuistry, to murder for my own sake, for myself alone! I didn't want to lie about it even to myself. It wasn't to help my mother I did the murder – that's nonsense – I didn't do the murder to gain wealth and power. Nonsense! I simply did it; I did the murder for myself, for myself alone … And it was not the money I wanted, Sonia, when I did it. It was not so much the money I wanted, but something else … I know it all now … Understand me! Perhaps I should never have committed a murder again. I wanted to find out something else; it was something else led me on. I wanted to find out then and quickly whether I was a louse like everybody else or a man. Whether I can step over barriers or not, whether I dare stoop to pick up or not, whether I am a trembling creature or whether I have the *right* …'

'To kill? Have the right to kill?' Sonia clasped her hands.

Hermeneutic Question What does Raskolnikov mean by 'the right to kill'?

Questions to take you further

* Are all people divided into 'ordinary' and 'extraordinary'?

* Should all people be judged by the same standards?

* Is there such a thing as genius?

* Are heroes real?

* Are some people larger than the society they live in?

* Does society limit us?

* Ralph Waldo Emerson wrote, 'No law can be sacred to me but that of my nature.' Do you agree?

Task Question 1 Does anyone have the right to break the law?

Questions to take you further

* Did Raskolnikov have the right to break the law?

* Should we trust our own conscience above all else?

* Should we follow the rules of the society we live in?

* If you have the right to make a law, do you have the right to break it?

* Where do rights come from?

* Are our rights defined by the law?

* What gives the law the right to dictate to us?

Raskolnikov thought that the law did not apply to extraordinary people. Even though the law may say a particular action is wrong, it isn't really. We only believe it is wrong because that is what the law dictates.

Task Question 2   Without the law would there still be right and wrong?

Questions to take you further

❖ Is morality something we discover or invent?

❖ If it is discovered, how is it discovered? Through our senses? Our conscience? Our instinct?

❖ If it is invented, what is its function?

❖ Is the law a necessary muzzle on our immoral hearts? Are we innately immoral?

❖ Should the law prohibit everything that is wrong?

This and the following Task Questions are searching for the ultimate source of value. You may hear answers to the effect that there would still be right and wrong because there is a God, or because we have rights, or because we can suffer. Each of these can act as the x in the next Task Question. Repeat the question till you reach a point where there is no longer right and wrong (or, to bypass repetition, bring out the first bullet point).

Task Question 3   Without x would there still be right and wrong?

Questions to take you further

❖ What would you have to remove from the world for right and wrong to no longer exist?

❖ How do we develop the idea that there is a difference between the way the world is and the way it ought to be?

❖ What is it within us that refuses to accept the world as it is? What is it within us that accepts the world as it is?

* What does it mean to value something? Why is it that we value things? What is the first thing in life that we value?

* Could we live without morality?

* What is morality?

Money

Surely the class issue has actually been successfully resolved in the West.

Francis Fukuyama

Imagine an alien visiting Earth. On its home planet there is no such thing as money.

Starter Question What do you think the alien would find confusing about money?

Questions to take you further

* What is money?

* Why is money desired? Why don't babies desire it?

* Why are humans the only animals with money?

* Why do some people have more than others? Why is it not shared?

* Is money a reward?

* Why do those with more money have more power in society?

* If people devote their lives to it, does that make it a religion?

He is a world-class striker playing for one of the greatest football clubs. He has been the league's top scorer for three seasons running. He was essential to his club winning the Champion's League. His name can be found on the backs of football shirts all over the world. Though his fans adore him, his teammates do not.

This player's salary is nearly double that of his teammates'. His enormous wealth allows him to lead a life of unimaginable extravagance and luxury. There is nearly nothing he can't buy. His fellow teammates, however, think this is unfair. They believe that every player should be paid the same amount.

Deciding to take action, the players go on strike. They refuse to either play or train till the club gives every player in the team equal pay.

The club, however, does not have enough money to pay the whole team as much as it does their 'star player'. They are considering reducing his earnings by nearly 50% and sharing this sum out among the rest of the team. That way the team's pay would be equal.

Task Question 1   Should the club do this?

Questions to take you further

* Does the most talented player deserve the highest pay?
* Does the hardest working player deserve the highest pay?
* Do some people deserve more than others?
* Is it possible to deserve too much?
* Does it matter if some people earn extraordinary amounts? Is it any of our business?
* Do footballers earn too much? Is there such a thing as earning too much?

Imagine that the club decides to level the pay. The star player takes a large pay cut, the other players have a slight pay rise and everyone in the team now receives an equal salary.

But the actions taken by these extraordinarily rich players have made other people think.

The locker-room staff feel that they are also part of the team: they wash the players' shirts, they polish their boots, they clean and tidy their changing room. If the players believe that everyone on the team should be paid equally, doesn't that mean that they should be paid the same as the players?

The players are paid 200 times as much as the locker-room staff. They live in mansions and drive luxury cars. They receive the best healthcare. They send their children to private schools. The locker-room staff, on the other hand, struggle to pay their rent, they struggle to heat their houses, they struggle to support their children. Because of these struggles, this harder life, they will probably die, on average, ten years younger than the wealthy footballers they clean for.

The locker-room staff believe that this is unfair. After all, they are all on the same team. So they go on strike. They tell the club that they will return to work once it has promised to give everyone on the team equal pay.

Of course, the club cannot afford to pay them as much as the players, so it would have to cut the players' pay by 90% and then share that money out. The players would be significantly worse off, but the cleaners would have enough money to lead comfortable lives and provide comfortable lives for their families, and everyone at the club would share the same pay.

Task Question 2   Should the club do this?

Questions to take you further

❖ Are the locker-room staff part of the team?

❖ Are footballers special, superior?

* Do the players' families deserve the luxury they receive?
* Do the families of the locker-room staff deserve their struggles?
* Is sharing essentially good?
* Can economic inequality be fair?
* Is poverty necessarily bad?

Imagine that the club does decide to do this. Its actions make the headlines and the conversation grows.

Throughout the country workers are beginning to question whether it's fair that their bosses are paid far more than they are. Inspired by the words of the football staff, they say to one another, 'We're part of the same team, aren't we? We're all part of this thing called the economy. Everyone on the team should be paid equally. Why should some struggle while others flourish? How can it be right that some have too little while others have too much?'

Workers throughout the country go on strike. Businesses grind to a halt. Shops close. The transport system collapses. Rubbish bags pile up in the street. The workers say that they will return to work once the government has ensured that all people are given equal pay.

Task Question 3   Should the government do this?

Questions to take you further

* Is everyone part of the same team?
* What is our team? Is it our nationality? Our economy? Our humanity?
* Are we all separate individuals? Should we care about the lives of strangers?
* Are some people more valuable than others? Valuable to whom?
* Does a person's pay reflect their value?

- ❖ If everyone were paid the same, what would our idea of a 'successful' job be?

- ❖ Are all people equal? What is it we share that makes us equal?

- ❖ Can inequality be good?

- ❖ Do we need hierarchies?

Street Art

I just don't see how a world that makes such wonderful things could be bad.

Ariel, The Little Mermaid

Starting with examples of street art, you might Google Andrew Schoultz and Aaron Noble's San Francisco mural, Generator, *to show the class. Or Gajin Fujita's work. Or look at the street artists they like.*

Generator *was actually commissioned by the owners of the house, but Schoultz also made clandestine murals, till the day he was caught and told to remove his picture. He never imagined it would happen like that: 'I always thought that if I was caught in the process of painting a really beautiful mural, the landlord would be like, "This is bitchin! Please proceed."'*

A kid has been caught by the police spray-painting pictures of flying giraffes and trumpet-playing blue birds on the side of a house. A policeman orders him to put the cans down. The kid tells him to hold on a minute while he finishes up.

On the drive to the police station.

Policeman You seem sort of slow in the head – don't make a policeman wait. Most of you lot have the good sense not to spray your crap in broad daylight.

Kid The wall bored me. I did you a favour.

Policeman It's vandalism.

Kid What?

Policeman It's vandalism. You deliberately ruined the building.

Kid That's your opinion. I think I did a great job.

Policeman No, it's not my opinion. It's the law. You don't have the right to interfere with other people's property.

Kid Yeah, I know.

Policeman And you did it anyway?

Kid I don't have the right to interfere with other people's property, sure, but that wall isn't someone else's property. It's mine.

Policeman How exactly is it yours? Somebody paid good money for it. It's their house.

Kid You think that wall is the outside of the owner's house, right? It's not. That wall is the inside of our street. I see that wall every day.

Policeman That wall belongs to the house, which belongs to the owner, who now has to pay to get it cleaned. And he'll have to see your ugly scribble every day till he does.

Kid Those houses are ugly. You know they tore down a half-pipe to build them. Where that guy's kitchen is, with his bar stools and his giant fridge, that's where me and my friends used to pass the time. I didn't ask for these houses. No one did. Who's to say the buildings aren't vandalism?

Policeman Vandalism?! They were approved by the council! They are family homes.

Kid Well, this street is my home. That wall is my home. I don't care if you want to vandalise my city with buildings just so long as I get to give them some colour.

Policeman The city is for families and businesses, it's made by honest people – people who work hard and do the right thing.

Kid Difference is, you want the street to be a prison, I want it to be a gallery. You want walls to be dividing lines, things that lock us out and the owners in. Because it doesn't matter whether we're the ones locked in or out, when there are dividing lines, it's all the same, everyone's locked up.

Policeman You're boring me now, kid.

Kid Art is about replacing stuff you hate with stuff you love. I hated that wall, now I love it. You don't love anything except law and order. I love beauty. And beauty can't stand law and order. You can't control it. All I'm saying is give beauty a chance, you know?

Policeman Kid, your little cartoon isn't beauty. It's not art. It's just some stupid doodle you made up. Art is serious business. It lasts. Like the *Mona Lisa*. It's not something that gets tagged over or left to fade in the sun.

Kid I'm serious about doodling. And I don't really see the difference between me and da Vinci, except that I'm alive.

It'd be fun to have the class dramatise the dialogue. Ask them to read through and act out the dialogue together in pairs. Have them think about their characters: how they would sit, talk, where they would look, gestures they would make, etc. Encourage them to ad lib, to respond to the arguments their adversaries make with their own in-character thoughts and ideas. Select a pair to perform for the class (a photocopiable version of this is available in Appendix 3).

Task Question 1 Are you on the kid's side or the policeman's? Is it wrong to graffiti on houses?

Questions to take you further

* Is the wall of a house the outside of the owner's property or the inside of a street?

* Who owns a street? Who owns a city?

* Do buildings have the right to bore us?

* Buildings are erected without our consent. Is it wrong to decorate them without consent?

* Is graffiti vandalism?

* The policeman is speaking on behalf of the law. Does that make him right?

* Graffiti involves people competing to exhibit and articulate their visions of a public space. Should democracies not celebrate and encourage this practice?

As well as returning to the dialogue for points of contention or illumination, you could also use Schoultz and Noble's Generator as a specimen and ask: would it be wrong if someone did this to your house? Would it be wrong even if you happened to love the picture?

Task Question 2 Are buildings vandalism?

Questions to take you further

❖ If so, are we entitled to destroy them? Can you vandalise vandalism?

❖ Are they vandalism if they are ugly and boring? What are they vandalising?

❖ If a building serves a good purpose, can it be vandalism?

❖ What is vandalism?

Use a few concrete – glass and steel, more likely – examples as reference points. Something local, maybe new. Maybe something abominable like The Shard. Anecdotally, you might mention that the Eiffel Tower was widely regarded as vandalism by Parisians when it was first built. A writer, Maupassant, hated the Tower so much he frequently dined in its restaurant; that was the only place in Paris he didn't have to see it.

Task Question 3 Is graffiti art?

Questions to take you further

❖ Can vandalism be art?

❖ What does calling it art entitle it to? How does it change the way we look at it?

❖ Should it be preserved and protected?

❖ Is this a question that should be left to curators and experts to decide?

❖ Who owns graffiti?

Consumerism

You can only spend so much money. What are you going to do? Have two lunches?

Neil Diamond

Select an advert for a popular product. Present it to the class and ask:

Starter Question 1   How does this advert try to make us want its product?

Steer the class's focus towards the desires that the advert attempts to arouse in the consumer, asking why it doesn't simply describe the product's functions. If it is said, for example, that the bright colours grab our attention, you might ask, 'Why are we attracted to bright colours? What does this say about our desires? What would it say about us if we were attracted to darker, quieter colours?'

Starter Question 2   Why do so many people want this product?

If answers are given that simply list the technical qualities of the product, follow this up by asking why someone would want something with these qualities, and keep pursuing with 'whys' till you hit some kind of bedrock. (Bedrock? Yes, one way of thinking about this might be Freud's: he suggested that people only ever really want the things they wanted as babies, so the 'bedrock' would be the point at which their description of the product sounds like something a baby might want.) If it is said that the product is desired for the status it confers (the envy it inspires), enquire as to why owning something of this sort confers status, i.e. what does it say about us? (If the status is suggested to relate to wealth, ask why buying, say, a very expensive hammer wouldn't accrue the same attention.)

Adverts do not simply report the qualities and usefulness of a product. They seem to appeal to something else besides or beyond our common sense. In 1903 the first book on the psychology of advertising was published by an American called Walter Dill Scott. This was the beginning of the science of consumer desire. Scott argued that consumers do not act rationally and therefore they can be easily influenced to spend their money. He thought that humans were fundamentally suggestible, that is to say, we do as we are told.

Picture adverts, he advised, must be of specific proportions, size and colour, because this will bring pleasure to the consumer, and the more pleasure we feel the more suggestible we are. Because we have this pliable nature, the best kind of advert is one that gives a short subtle command, for example, 'Let iPhone make your day.' This command would work even better if accompanied by a picture of someone, because we will then think it is this person who is making the command. If somebody instructs us, we will dutifully obey.

As people started to consume more in the 20th century, advertising companies started to employ psychologists. They believed that understanding the workings of the mind would be useful in marketing products. John B. Watson was one such psychologist. He believed that humans were governed by three basic emotions: love, fear and rage. By appealing to those emotions it would be possible to make people do nearly anything. He thought that adverts could be used as ways of training people to shop.

An example of an advert shaped by his ideas was one for toothpaste. The advert depicted an attractive woman smoking and explained that this particular brand of toothpaste would prevent her developing stained teeth and bad breath. The advert was an attempt to make the consumer purchase the toothpaste out of the fear of becoming ugly. Adverts might also repeatedly show the product in connection with something desirable, say, a brand of juice that is drunk on a warm beach. If we are repeatedly exposed to this advert, we will begin to associate the juice with the beach, and so the juice will, by association, arouse in us the same feelings of pleasure as the beach does. These ideas and methods are now very familiar to us.

Today there is an entire industry of research into ways of influencing us to spend money. The lighting, smells and background music of shops are designed to turn us into consumers. Research has shown that we will spend more money in flower shops where love songs are played and more in wine shops where classical music is played; we will also spend more money specifically on French wine if the music is French. The tempo of background music is also effective. If the music played in cafés has a fast rather than a slow tempo, we will take more bites per minute.

Task Question 1   Do we want the things we buy or are we made to want them?

Questions to take you further

- ❖ Can we be forced to want things?
- ❖ Can we want things we don't really want?
- ❖ What does it mean to 'really' want something?
- ❖ How can we tell which of our wants are real and which are fake?
- ❖ Are we suggestible?
- ❖ Is there such a thing as a self-determined consumer?
- ❖ Do adverts exploit us? Are they unethical?
- ❖ Are we a product of our culture?

Aldous Huxley's 1932 novel, *Brave New World,* describes a society in which everybody gets what they want and nobody wants what they can't get. In this society happiness prevails; unhappiness is regarded as a historical curiosity. If people ever experience boredom, anxiety or anger, they simply take a drug called soma. Soma is legal

and actively encouraged by the state. It comforts and consoles; it returns one to a state of peace and stability. Soma, it is believed, eradicates the need for religion.

The society of *Brave New World* is consumerist. This means that its economy depends upon its citizens' constant purchasing of products and services. For this reason everyone is taught to continuously desire more, to discard their old possessions and always seek the newest goods. These ideas are summarised in slogans, such as 'Ending is better than mending', which are conditioned into the populace from infancy via a process called 'Sleep Teaching'. To ensure the society's compliance with its consumerist underpinnings, recorded messages are played into the ears of sleeping children that dictate what they should think and what they should want. These messages sink deep into their minds and will subconsciously govern their entire lives.

The primary aim of this society is stability. A cocktail of consumerism and soma guarantees the total elimination of frustration. In this society nobody waits for anything. As soon as they sense the stirrings of desire, they relieve it with shopping or travelling or drugs. Patience is not a virtue but an expendable bane. People are universally happy; they get what they want, and they never want what they can't get. They are safe. Affluence and ease are the order of things.

Task Question 2 Is this world a reflection of our own?

Questions to take you further

❖ Are we encouraged to consume?

❖ What pleasures does society encourage us to pursue?

❖ What is our society's idea of a good life?

❖ Do we consume too much? Are we greedy? Is this a vice?

❖ Do shopping centres make people happier?

❖ Do shopping centres make people deader?

- Is advertising similar to 'Sleep Teaching'?
- Does our society use anything like soma?
- Do we all desire happiness?
- If you were offered a credit card you never had to pay off, would you take it? Why?

With the third bullet point, you could first ask the class to describe their ideas of a good life, of the kinds of lives they want. This would be an interesting discussion in itself: to consider their beliefs about what makes a life worth living. You could then tie it back to the dystopian theme by seeing if there are any overlaps and commonalities between the pupils' various conceptions, and then wonder why different people share the same ideals. Are these commonalities reflective of our innate humanity? Are they merely coincidences? Or are they a result of enculturation? And if they are a result of enculturation, how does this process work? How do we become socialised? You might also ask whether they think there is anything wrong with wanting what the culture tells you to want. Is this compliance or belonging?

Task Question 3   Is happiness good?

Questions to take you further

- Should soma be available to us?
- Is there such a thing as too much happiness?
- Is there such a thing as too little happiness?
- Are there better things than happiness?
- Do we need to suffer? Is pain ever good?
- What is happiness?
- Is comfort good? Should we try to make our lives as comfortable as possible?
- Are discomfort, frustration or anxiety ever good?

It might be said that it would be boring to be constantly happy. You could respond to this by asking whether we would be bored at the same time as being happy. If that's not possible, then does it follow that perpetual happiness is actually unimaginable? What is it about us that precludes our settling into this eternal state? On the other hand, if it's said that boredom and happiness can coexist, is this because happiness is actually a form of boredom? Or because there are different parts of the mind capable of inhabiting conflicting states? Taking a different line, it could also be asked whether there would be anything wrong with missing out on boredom (see 'Desire'), whether there is value in boredom, and what other states being permanently happy would cause us to miss out on. How high is happiness on the list of desirable states?

Power

'I ought to be chief,' said Jack with simple arrogance, 'because I'm chapter chorister and head boy. I can sing C sharp.'

William Golding

Starter Question   What is power?

Questions to take you further

❖ Why do some people have more power than others?

❖ Who has power over you?

❖ Do you have enough power?

❖ Is power good?

❖ Is there such a thing as too much power?

❖ Are humans the most powerful animal?

❖ Are there limits to power?

❖ Are all people vulnerable?

❖ Is there anyone that is powerless?

You can investigate this question by splitting the board into two columns, one headed 'Possessed' and the other 'Lacking', and ask the class to think of the powers they have and the powers they don't. You might also ask the class to think of the world's most powerful people, and then its most powerful person, wondering what the nature of this power is.

I would recommend allowing pupils to read the following dialogues individually before discussing them. Whereas the other dialogues in the book lend themselves to performance, these would benefit from close reading. Ask the class to underline and annotate any particular points of agreement or disagreement (a photocopiable version of this is available in Appendix 4).

A I've been wondering what sort of people should rule society.

B Do you think the worst people should rule society?

A Well, no, that's a ridiculous idea.

B So should the best people rule society?

A Yes.

B Would criminals be the best people?

A Certainly not.

B Would people who do not know anything about politics be best?

A No, otherwise they wouldn't know what they were doing.

B So the best people should have studied politics?

A Yes, that seems right.

B Does it follow, then, that the best people should have studied politics at the best places?

A Yes, it does follow.

B And would the best people be those whose opinions aren't clouded by their own personal experiences?

A I should think so. Then they will be fair.

B And isn't it true that the poorest people in society are often the most resentful?

A Yes, you see that.

B So are the poorest people the most likely to be well-balanced and impartial?

A No.

B So should the best people be poor or should they be of a comfortable class?

A I suppose they should be comfortable.

B Would you expect also that the best people would have the best understanding of the society they are ruling?

A I would expect that, just as you'd want a captain to have a thorough understanding of her ship.

B So the best people, those with the best understanding, should know about the society's history?

A Yes.

B Would you further agree that those who have grown up within the society's oldest institutions would have the best understanding of it?

A That seems right.

B So, given what we've said, would you conclude that the best people to rule a society are those who have attended the oldest schools, been educated at the best universities and come from well-off families?

A I would conclude that.

Task Question 1   Do you accept this conclusion?

For those who do accept the conclusion, their reasons for doing so may already be present within the dialogue, so when you start the discussion it would be good to specifically ask whether anyone rejects the conclusion. Those who do accept it will then have something to think through, namely, why the dissenters are wrong.

A I've been wondering what sort of people should rule society.

B Do you think the worst people should rule society?

A Well, no, that's a ridiculous idea.

B So should the best people rule society?

A Yes.

B Would the best people preserve the worst things about society?

A Of course not.

B So the best people would be those who are most capable of correcting the worst things about society?

A Yes, a society has no chance of being the best it can without changing what is worst about it.

B Would you agree that one of the worst aspects of any society is poverty?

A I can't think of anyone who would disagree with that.

B Do you think it's true that to correct something you need to understand it?

A That seems right.

B And who do you think understands poverty more, the rich or the poor?

A The poor, of course.

B Do you also think that the poor would have the most desire to correct poverty?

A Certainly.

B So they would have the most cause to change the worst things about society?

A Yes.

B Are university lecturers poor?

A No, they are quite well-off.

B Would they be able to teach you about poverty?

A I don't think so. Universities are not poor places.

B So are universities the best places to teach you about society?

A It doesn't seem so.

B Would you say that the best people should be those who are most able to make society new?

A Yes, those who can change it and make it better.

B Who would you say is most able to make society new: those who respect the past or those who disrespect it?

A Those who disrespect it, obviously.

B And would you say that those who least respect the past are those who have grown up within society's oldest institutions?

A I wouldn't say that, old institutions don't like change.

B So, given what we've said, would you conclude that the best people to rule a society are those who have not attended the oldest schools or been educated at university, but those who come from poor circumstances and have the least respect for the past?

A I would conclude that.

Task Question 2   Do you accept this conclusion?

Question to take you further

❖ What attributes should politicians have?

For as long as it's been in use, 'anarchist' has seemingly been a term of abuse, dismissal or fear. Meaning 'without a ruler', the word today still connotes chaos and nihilism. Yet in 1840 it underwent a significant reinvention by Pierre-Joseph Proudhon. Refusing to be stereotyped and silenced by the word, he said of himself, 'I am an anarchist', and so turned a sign of contempt into a mark of conviction.

Anarchists believe that society should exist without government. They are against all forms of state control: laws, courts, prisons, the army, etc. They believe that government is oppressive, that it primarily serves the interests of the rich. Government maintains social inequality whilst encouraging mindless conformity. To be governed is to be enslaved. Anarchists do not believe in hierarchy, power or authority. They believe that society is capable of running itself without external interference. Rather than being managed, workers can organise themselves collectively. Rather than being taxed to help the needy, we can volunteer our charity. Anarchists believe that government divides society; that we would flourish without it.

Proudhon articulated ideas of this kind. His brief time in politics led him to conclude that 'fear of the people is the sickness of all those who belong to authority; the people, for those in power, are the enemy'. While some of his books were censored by the French government, others were not because they were deemed too complicated to be understood by the general public. This is a passage from Proudhon that his readers had no difficulty understanding:

To be governed is to be watched over, inspected, spied on, directed, legislated, regimented, closed in, indoctrinated, preached at, controlled, assessed, evaluated, censored, commanded; all by creatures that have neither the right, nor wisdom, nor virtue ... To be governed means that at every move, operation, or transaction one is noted, registered, entered in a census, taxed, stamped, priced, assessed, patented, licensed, authorized, recommended, admonished, prevented, reformed, set right, corrected ... at the first sign of resistance or word of complaint, one is repressed, fined, despised, vexed, pursued, hustled, beaten up, garrotted, imprisoned, shot, machine-gunned, judged, sentenced, deported, sacrificed, sold, betrayed, and to cap it all, ridiculed, mocked, outraged, and dishonoured. *That* is government, *that* is its justice and its morality!

Task Question 3   Do we need rulers?

Questions to take you further

❖ Is it wrong for some people to have more power than others?

❖ Should society give us more power than we actually have?

- Are we oppressed?

- Could social peace be achieved through means other than law and punishment?

- Proudhon once said, 'Anarchy is order.' What could this mean?

- Is peace compatible with freedom?

- Are we too irresponsible to live without rulers?

- Are we helpless without authority?

- What is authority?

- Who can we trust?

Pupils may object to anarchism for Hobbesian reasons, believing that the removal of the state will exacerbate the level of crime already present in society. Here you can explore their ideas about what crime is and why people commit it. Would there be less crime if there were more equality? If people didn't feel politically invisible? If cooperation were seen as a good? You can then look at whether the state is responsible for inequality, invisibility and individualism.

Tradition and Change

A living dog is better than a dead lion.

Ecclesiastes 9:4

Many schools and universities use mottos to express their ideals and establish their identity. The motto of New College, Oxford, founded in 1379, is 'Manners Makyth Man'.

Hermeneutic Question   What do you think this means?

Question to take you further

❖ Why would a college want this as their motto?

Prior to its Revolution, France existed under the rule of
King Louis XVI. He was the supreme power, answerable
to no one, able to make and repeal laws at will. But there
was a desire in France for change; the revolutionaries sought
to overturn monarchy, hierarchy and privilege. From 1789,
with the storming of the Bastille (the first public uprising), to
1793, France was transformed from an absolute monarchy to
a republic. King Louis and Marie Antoinette were decapitated,
feudalism and the nobility were abolished, the *ancien régime* was swept
away. The revolutionaries introduced a new flag, they invented a new
state religion – the cult of the Supreme Being – and they instated a new
calendar, which defined 1792, the year the Republic was declared, as
year 1, the beginning of time. The revolutionaries were not interested
in merely escaping the past; they positively sought to erase it.

The Revolution was in part a revolution of manners. The vociferous
sans-culotte were a group of revolutionaries who prided themselves on
their lack of aristocratic manners. Their name, *sans-culotte*, meaning
'without knee-breeches', referred to their opposition to aristocratic
dress. They were against what they called 'respectable people'. If you
were found speaking with or demanding respect, they would denounce
you. They would reprimand anyone asking to be called sir; elegance
was regarded as a criminal offence. The *sans-culotte* believed that pride
and dignity were enemies of the fraternal spirit of the new republic.

Across the Channel in England, Edmund Burke was a bun-
dle of nerves. He was passionately opposed to the
revolution in France and expressed his worries in a
remarkably eloquent tantrum, *Reflections on the
Revolution in France*. What he couldn't bear to see was

the tragic degradation of manners. 'The age of chivalry is gone,' he moaned.

Burke believed that manners were more important to society than laws because manners are diffuse, in the air we breathe, determining the quality and tenor of our lives together. Manners shield us from barbarism. Without duty, reverence and respect civilisation would fall apart. Watching the changes in France, he wrote:

The age of chivalry is gone ... Never, never more, shall we behold that generous loyalty to rank and sex, that proud submission, that dignified obedience, that subordination of the heart.

The decent drapery of life is to be rudely torn off ... necessary to cover the defects of our naked shivering nature, and to raise it to dignity. On this scheme of things, a king is but a man; a queen is but a woman; a woman is but an animal; and an animal not of the highest order.

There ought to be a system of manners in every nation which a well-formed mind would be disposed to relish. To make us love our country, our country ought to be lovely. Nothing is more certain, than that our manners, our civilisation, have depended upon two principles – the spirit of a gentleman, and the spirit of religion.

Task Question 1 Are manners as important as Burke believes?

Questions to take you further

❖ Do we need manners?

❖ Do we need dignity?

- Is respect important? Do we need it?

- Is obedience a virtue?

- Is there a barbarian within us? Is civilisation precarious?

- Do we need a figure we can look up to, a figure that can look down on us?

- Would we be lost without a sense of propriety?

- Is duty good?

- What are manners? What is dignity?

Burke was an anti-revolutionary. He wrote, 'When the ancient opinions and rules of life are taken away, the loss cannot possibly be estimated. From that moment we have no compass to govern us ... Good order is the foundation of all good things.'

He believed that we should honour tradition because it is very much larger than we are. Though we perish, it endures. We should not, and cannot, change everything without committing the greatest violence against ourselves. We are defined by our traditions; tradition is what makes us fully human. We would be lost without it. We can't just wipe everything away and start again. A blank slate is a void. Social problems should be treated like 'the wounds of a father'; to be approached with 'awe and trembling', not blithe disregard.

Task Question 2   Do we need tradition?

Questions to take you further

- Should revolutionary change be avoided? Is prudence a virtue?

- Is there such a thing as too much change?

- Do we need a home? Is tradition like home?

- Are we defined by tradition, by the culture we live in?

- Is tradition an obstacle to the future? Does it impede progress?

- ❖ William Blake wrote, 'Expect poison from the standing water.' What might this say about tradition?

- ❖ Is it possible to erase the past?

- ❖ Do we need the past?

- ❖ Is good order the foundation of all good things?

- ❖ Imagine a society that wanted to burn every book ever written in order to start afresh and write new works, works unencumbered by the literature and ideas of the past. Would this be a good idea?

Before or in the midst of discussing these questions, you could ask the class to think of the traditions that form parts of their lives. Why do we like doing things the same way over and over? What is the purpose of these traditions? Why are they important to us? Should they be preserved? Examples might include Christmas, New Year's Eve (is celebrating the start of something new with the same old traditions a lavish stab at irony?), birthdays, Sunday lunch, as well as more personal ones. Pupils who express no commitment to tradition can become somewhat ambivalent when fictional instances are raised; for example, would there be anything wrong with modernising Hogwarts, with demolishing and reconstructing the building in order to make it more energy efficient and better suited to the demands of the 21st century? This question could be related to the proposals in the 1960s – commissioned by the government and delivered by the architect Leslie Martin – to demolish the 'anachronistic' Foreign Office on Whitehall and Middlesex Guildhall and replace them with buildings concrete and modern.

Traditions are shared, they constitute so-called communities. The wish to throw off tradition and depart from the past can be a wish to become an individual, something new and separate.

Task Question 3   Is it better to be an individual or a member of a community?

Questions to take you further

- Is the individual an isolate?

- Is community a prison?

- Is it possible to be both?

- What is it more natural for us to be?

- Are we all defined more by our differences or our similarities?

Race

Each individual is an isolate, permanently non-communicating,
permanently unknown, in fact unfound.

D. W. Winnicott

Starter Question 1   What is race?

Questions to take you further

- What races are there? What defines them?

- Is race more than skin-deep?

- Is race biological?

- Is race psychological?

- Is race sociological?

- Do you have a race? Is it possible to have no race at all?

Imagine that tomorrow the people of the world wake up identical. Everyone will be green and share the same physical features.

Starter Question 2   Would it be possible to identify which race people were?

The concept of race is an old one which historically has gone hand-in-hand with the belief in a natural hierarchy of humans. The idea that nature has arranged humankind into distinct groups is used to justify acts of brutality against those deemed naturally inferior. It was Thomas Jefferson, the third president of the United States, who in one breath told us that all men are created equal, and in the next explained how between master and slave there were insoluble racial differences. 'Blacks', he said, are 'inferior to the whites in the endowments both of body and mind ... In imagination, they are dull, tasteless, and anomalous ... Their griefs are transient ... They secrete less by the kidnies.'

Race was a concept used in America to explain why, despite universal equality, some (the slaves) were not quite as equal as the rest. People were not enslaved because of their race; the idea of race was called upon to justify their slavery.

The belief in natural hierarchies led to eugenics, a pseudoscience which seeks to control reproduction in order to create perfect people. Francis Galton, the founder of eugenics, believed, for example, in a hierarchy of intelligence. He claimed that the ancient Greeks were one grade more intelligent than the English, who were two grades more intelligent than 'Negroes', who were one grade more intelligent than Aboriginal Australians, who were eight grades more intelligent than dogs. These ideas were adopted by the Nazis in their quest for a 'Master Race', but they were already being implemented in the US.

For many decades in the 20th century, compulsory sterilisation was practised in numerous states, with California having the most egregious record. In order to filter out the 'feeble minded' and purify our biological stock, many thousands of people in America had their ability to reproduce forcibly taken from them. This was an inspiration to the Nazis.

Though the belief in eugenics and natural hierarchies has waned, the belief in race has not. There is, however, no scientific basis to the concept. It used to be thought that race was a matter of blood, that one's blood could be used to identify one's race; the Red Cross, for example, has been known to segregate 'black blood' from 'white blood'. But as the British anthropologist Ashley Montagu has explained, 'the blood of all human beings is in every respect the same, with only one exception, that is, in the agglutinating properties of the blood which yields the four blood groups. But these agglutinating properties and the four blood groups are present in all varieties of men, and in various groups of men they differ only in their statistical distribution. There are no known or demonstrable differences in the character of the blood of different peoples. The blood of the Negro is identical with that of all other human beings, so that for purposes of transfusion, or any other purposes, it is as good as any other blood.'

It has also been suggested that the hereditary blood disorder, sickle cell anaemia, which can be found in some Africans, is a signifier of racial difference. But this disorder is environmental, not racial. It is found in populations that live in tropical areas such as Western Africa, the Middle East, the Persian Gulf, the Mediterranean and India. The sickle cell trait provides its carrier with a better chance of surviving malaria, which is a disease typical of the tropics.

Just as blood cannot support the concept of race, nor can genes. Africans tend to be identified as belonging to the 'black race', but Africa has a greater genetic diversity than any other area on the planet. A person from Nigeria and a person from Kenya are likely to be more genetically different from each other than either is to a person from Ireland.

Physical traits fail to define race because local populations produce traits that adapt to climate and other environmental factors. However genetically or geographically distant they are, tropical populations will have physical traits that match tropical conditions, like the sickle cell message; Kenyans and Peruvians will have greater lung capacities and red blood cell counts from living at high altitudes.

We might identify race by physical characteristics such as skin colour. But then why not say that tall people or people with curly hair constitute separate races? The lack of a scientific basis led Ashley Montagu to compare the belief in race to the belief in witchcraft. Race, he said, is the witchcraft of our time; it is 'humankind's most dangerous myth'.

Task Question 1   Is race an illusion?

Questions to take you further

* Is it a reasonable, albeit false, belief?
* Has nature arranged humankind into distinct groups?
* Are we all fundamentally alike or are we all wildly different?
* Are some people ineluctably foreign? Ineluctably different?
* Does our physical appearance define us?
* Is the belief in race like the belief in witchcraft?
* Without the concept of race, how would you describe what racism is?
* Is believing the illusion a matter of stupidity?

Starter Question 3   Besides 'race', what other ways do we have of categorising people?

Task Question 2   Are there any legitimate ways to categorise people?

Questions to take you further

* Can we know a lot about a person by knowing their category?
* Is prejudice ever legitimate?

* Are categories necessary?

* Do we have identities?

* What defines us?

Democracy and Difference

Of course it was wrong to want to change people, but what else could you possibly want to do with them?

Edward St Aubyn

In 1989, in a school in Creil, France, three Muslim pupils were expelled for refusing to remove their hijabs. It was left to the Council of State to decide whether the expulsion was legal and it was ruled that pupils should not be refused admission for wearing headscarves, but the Council introduced a significant degree of ambiguity by forbidding 'ostentatious' religious clothing. Later that year in a suburb of Paris, 65 teachers refused to teach because there was a single pupil wearing a hijab (the pupil acquiesced and removed it). Similar incidents persisted.

In 1993, in a town near Lyon, the refusal of four girls to remove their hijabs during PE led to the majority of the school's teachers going on strike. In 1994, across different schools in different areas, over 70 girls were expelled for wearing the hijab. Some of these expulsions were subsequently overturned by the courts, but some were not.

Incidents like these received a great deal of media attention and political discussion, but interest in the issue somewhat subsided for a few years. Then, in 2003, two teenage girls, Alma and Lila Levy – whose parents are atheists – were expelled from their school in a suburb of

Paris for, once again, not complying with school orders to remove their hijabs.

The girls were accustomed to ignoring the school's repeated injunctions against their headscarves, but the day they arrived with their ears, hairline and neck covered, it was the school's view that their clothing now constituted, in the words of the Council, 'an act of pressure, provocation, proselytism or propaganda'.

Finally, in 2004, the French government voted in – with an overwhelming majority, and backed by a similarly overwhelming level of support from the public – a law that made it illegal to wear items of religious affiliation in schools, including the hijab, large Christian crosses, Sikh turbans and Jewish kippahs.

Hermeneutic Question   Why do you think the French government imposed this law?

If you note down several different suggested reasons, as a class you could then discuss which, if any, of these reasons seem like good reasons and which of them do not.

Task Question 1   Should religious clothing be banned in schools?

Questions to take you further

❖ Should we hide our differences for the sake of community and cohesion?

❖ Is religion a private affair?

❖ Are there things we should only do in private? What makes something a private affair?

❖ Will hiding our differences help us to be more tolerant of each other?

❖ Is community more important than freedom of expression?

* Are differences a threat to community?

* Is difference bad? Is there such a thing as too much difference? Is there such a thing as too little?

* Is conflict bad?

Focusing on the third bullet point, you could draw up a table with one column titled 'Public' and the other 'Private' and ask the class to think of examples of publicly tolerable and intolerable acts.

Questions regarding which people, and what forms of behaviour, are both acceptable and desirable within a public democratic arena obviously extends to suffrage. According to the Representation of the People Act 1983, convicted prisoners in the UK do not have the freedom to vote in parliamentary and local government elections. However, since 2005, the European Court of Human Rights (ECHR) has persistently told the UK to change its policy because prisoner disenfranchisement is a violation of human rights and is illegal.

In 2011 MPs supported a motion – by 234 votes to 22 – opposing the changes prescribed by the ECHR. The prime minister, David Cameron, commented, 'It makes me physically ill to even contemplate having to give the vote to anyone who is in prison. Frankly, when people commit a crime and they go to prison they should lose their rights, including the right to vote.'

Task Question 2   Should prisoners be allowed to vote?

Questions to take you further

* Do some people deserve not to be listened to?

* Is it silly to argue that prisoners should have the right to vote when they don't even have the right to take a walk? Why should they have some rights but not others?

- Is it consistent to believe in prisoner votes while believing in prison?
- Are prisoners members of society?
- Is prison a violation of human rights? Or is crime a self-imposed surrender of them?
- Can we lose our rights?

Imagine you are a democratically elected leader. The next election is drawing near, but your popularity is steadily falling. Throughout your term you have worked tirelessly to do what you believe is best for the country. However, due to a series of unprecedented environmental disasters, your efforts have been unsuccessful and the country is experiencing high levels of unemployment, crime and general unrest. The public are growing increasingly angry and eager for someone they can blame. Extremist solutions are growing in popularity. A rival political party has built its manifesto along such lines. One of its proposed policies is to reintroduce capital punishment. This idea has received widespread support from the public. You believe, however, that capital punishment is wrong; in fact, you know it is. You know that this party are the wrong party for the country. You know they are motivated by fear and bloodlust, but they are leading in the polls and their success is almost certain. To prevent the public from committing what you see as a catastrophic mistake, you are considering declaring a state of emergency whereby the election will be indefinitely suspended. Until there is a lift in the country's fortunes, and the public is more able to vote in its own best interest, you will rule without consent.

Starter Question   Should you do this?

Questions to take you further

- If the public's attitudes never did change, would you rule this way permanently?
- Is democracy the best form of government?

❖ Is it always wrong to force other people to do as you wish?

❖ Is it wrong to want to control the world?

❖ What are the basic principles of democracy? Do you believe in them?

Task Question 3   Should everyone be allowed to vote?

Questions to take you further

❖ Should only those who perform competently at IQ tests be allowed to vote?

❖ Should only those with a sound moral pedigree be allowed to vote?

❖ Should only those who make a valuable contribution to society be allowed to vote?

❖ Are some people's political beliefs and opinions more valuable than others'?

❖ Should we tolerate people who hate tolerance?

❖ Are we violating our belief in tolerance if we don't tolerate them?

❖ Should racist people be allowed to vote?

❖ Should racist people be allowed to teach?

❖ Should we be free to express our views, whatever they are?

Others

'You'

The only form of lying that is absolutely beyond reproach is lying for its own sake.

Oscar Wilde

Animals

Only man can fall from God.

D. H. Lawrence

She is 4 years old with pure-black eyes. Her disposition is gentle. Despite her impressive bodily strength she would do you no harm. Most days she remains standing for hours in peace among her friends. Her friends are familiar to her and provide a sense of comfort. She needs this comfort for she is often fearful. Unfamiliar faces and scenes cause her heart to race, but she is intensely curious. Newness intrigues as well as terrifies her. She is always mindful of her surroundings. Her alertness can be put to rest with a tender scratch behind her ears. She is soothed by touch.

She is a mother and has twice given birth. Her young are always by her side. They feed from her milk, living through her body, nourished and sustained by it. She is admirably protective of them. If she senses they are in danger, she will do all she can to defend them. She is deeply aware of their vulnerability and this can be an acute source of worry for her. She would fight for their safety. She would throw herself into danger for them. Her young will depend on her stable care and attention for almost a year.

This is her last day of life.

Tomorrow she will be led onto a truck and taken away. At the journey's end, she will be guided from the truck down a snake of metallic passageways and forced into a tight container. The container will press down on her so that she cannot move.

Once she is fastened into place, a gun will be pointed at her head and a steel bolt will be fired into her skull. If she is lucky this will kill her instantly, but there is a good chance she will remain conscious. If she does remain conscious, she will experience having her back legs tied in chains and being hung upside down, suspended. She will feel herself being carried by a machine to a room where her throat will be slit. She will remain hanging as the blood drains out of her body. If she is still conscious, she will know that she is dying, and she will struggle. She will fight for her life, but she will lose. It will take several minutes for the blood to drain away. After this her body will be skinned.

They will cut her flesh into plate-sized portions and wrap it in plastic. Her packaged flesh will be displayed in supermarket aisles and exchanged for money. Different parts of her hacked body will be sold in numerous supermarkets and end up in the mouths of numerous people. These people will never know or meet one another. They will never know that they share her flesh in common, that her juices are inside each of their bodies. They will wash her down with a drink.

Her body is her living being. It is through her body that she exists. Tomorrow her body will be mutilated and sold. Particles of her flesh will be picked from the teeth of those who purchase her, of those who have never seen her pure-black eyes or felt the constant beating of her beating heart.

This story is shocking and ambiguous. Using the ambiguity to work through the shock, it would be good to open by asking what the class thinks the story is about. After letting the interpretations coalesce, you can then ask whether they think the story is opposed to what it describes, is against eating animals. If so, how can you tell? This question takes us into what the story feels and thereby raises the question of what it makes us feel, of the feelings it is trying to communicate, which leads into the Hermeneutic Question.

Hermeneutic Question   Is this story manipulative?

Questions to take you further

- ❖ Should moral arguments be settled with reason?

❖ Do we learn what is wrong and right through reason?

❖ Is the story forcing you to feel anything? Is it possible to force others to feel?

❖ Is it wrong to force others to believe what you do, even if you are right?

❖ Can stories be arguments?

❖ What's wrong with being manipulated?

The logical version of this question would be: Has the argument committed the argumentum ad misericordiam? This is Latin for 'argument to pity', and it is believed to be a fallacy, an attempt to reach a conclusion through irrational means, in this case through sympathy. Since it is not obvious that the story constitutes an argument, I haven't used the logical version. But you could ask the class to try and reconstruct the story as an argument (see Appendix 6). An analogous question to those raised in the bullet points would then be: is ad misericordiam really a fallacy?

To take a literary approach, you could ask the class to think about the rhetoric. Which words and sentences have the most power running through them? Then, to pose a philosophical question: is rhetoric a form of lying? Is there a more honest and less decorative way that the events could have been described? Is the emotion of the story in what is described or just in the description itself; is it in the events or the words, or is it impossible to separate events from words?

Task Question 1   Do animals have emotions?

Questions to take you further

❖ Do animals experience similar emotions to humans?

❖ Is it possible to sympathise with animals?

❖ Are humans animals?

❖ Do animals have reason?

- Of course animals are living, but do they have lives?
- What is a life?
- What are emotions?

If the story is inviting us to sympathise with the suffering of animals, it is presupposing that there are emotions there to be sympathised with. This is, in part, the pertinence of this question.

Task Question 2   Is it wrong to eat animals?

Questions to take you further

- Is it wrong to kill things with emotions?
- Is it natural for humans to eat animals?
- Are humans entitled to eat animals?
- Is killing an animal an act of murder?
- Is a person's appetite more valuable than an animal's life?
- Why is meat important to us? Why do people feel they *need* it? Why do they not feel they *need* salad?

The Sacred

Don't play with what lies deep in another person!

Ludwig Wittgenstein

Starter Question 1   Can you think of something we shouldn't do?

At this point take a somewhat trivial example of wrongness, say, littering or petty theft.

Starter Question 2   Is there any situation in which it wouldn't be wrong to do this?

Task Question   Is there anything we should *never* do?

1.   *Take an answer.*

2.   *Ask if anyone can think of a situation in which it would be permissible to perform that action. Ask whether, in this situation, the action would be merely acceptable or actually good.*

3.   *Allow for a discussion to develop on whether the situation does indeed justify or excuse the action.*

4.   *Then return to the Task Question and ask the class to think again of something that it would be wrong to do no matter what.*

5.   *Repeat steps 1–4 ad infinitum.*

Egoism

All my misfortunes come from my need to attach my heart.

Jean-Jacques Rousseau

For this session you'll need a deck of cards and three pairs of randomly selected volunteers.

Imagine that you and a friend have been caught flooding the school toilets. The teacher that catches you is a psychology teacher, Dr Z, and rather than simply punishing you, she wants to experiment on you.

Dr Z seats you opposite each other and gives you each one red card and one black card. She explains the rules:

✧   If you both play the red card, you both get an hour detention.

❖ If you play the black card and the other person plays the red card, you get to go home and they get a three-hour detention.

❖ If you play the red card and the other person plays the black card, you get a three-hour detention and they get to go home.

❖ If you both play the black card, you both get a two-hour detention.

Which card would you play?

Run the experiment three times with three different pairs of volunteers and record the results.

Hermeneutic Question 1   What, if anything, does this experiment prove about people?

Questions to take you further

❖ Does it prove that people are/are not selfish?

❖ Does the experiment create a situation that is similar to real life?

❖ Can artificial experiments teach us about human nature?

❖ Can science improve our understanding of human nature?

The following extract is taken from Richard Dawkins' book, *The Selfish Gene*.

If we were told that a man had lived a long and prosperous life in the world of Chicago gangsters, we would be entitled to make some guesses as to the sort of man he was. We might expect that he would have qualities such as toughness, a quick trigger finger, and the ability to attract loyal friends.

We, and all other animals, are machines created by our genes. Like successful Chicago gangsters, our genes have survived, in some cases for millions of years, in a highly competitive world.

This entitles us to expect certain qualities in our genes. A predominant quality to be expected in a successful gene is ruthless selfishness. This gene selfishness will usually give rise to selfishness in individual behaviour.

Humans and baboons have evolved by natural selection. If you look at the way natural selection works, it seems to follow that anything that has evolved by natural selection should be selfish. Therefore we must expect that when we go and look at the behaviour of baboons, humans, and all other living creatures, we shall find it to be selfish.

Hermeneutic Question 2   Why does Dawkins think that human behaviour must be selfish?

Questions to take you further

* Is his view based on science?

* Does his view appropriate science?

* Is his view an objective assessment?

* Is his view cynicism?

Task Question 1   Are people basically selfish?

Questions to take you further

* Do we act only to serve our own interests?

* Is life a competition? What are we competing for?

* Is selfishness a part of human nature?

* Are people able to change their nature?

* Are we able to generalise about all people?

- ❖ Is survival the primary aim in life? In order for us to survive must others perish?
- ❖ Can we learn about human nature by observing animal nature?
- ❖ Can we trust other people?
- ❖ Can cynicism be refuted?
- ❖ What is selfishness?
- ❖ What is selflessness?

Because this is in some sense a psychological question, when you ask why pupils think what they do, you are looking for evidence as well as reasons. You are looking for examples that prove or disprove human selfishness. A way to focus the discussion would be take some of these examples – say, giving to charity – and open them up to the class, asking for their interpretations of what it shows, e.g. is kindness hubris? Is charity more about alleviating guilt than doing good? Is this tedious cynicism? As well as seeking examples, tie answers back to the Dawkins excerpt by asking what in the passage they consent or object to.

The sad origin of echoes is explained in the Greek myth of Narcissus.

Narcissus was beautiful. There was always *someone* in love with him. Yet he spurned all the adoration he inspired. He wasn't interested in being fawned over. He was vaguely repulsed by the way he was doted on, and broken hearts trailed him like footprints.

Echo was a nymph who fell for the common snare of his beauty. She saw him walking alone one day through the countryside and was entranced. Secretly she followed him, feeling her heart stumble as she drew closer. But Echo suffered from a curse, a problem of speech, which Hera had inflicted upon her.

Hera, Zeus' wife (and twin-sister), had one day come close to finding him in bed with several nymphs, but she was stopped by Echo, who detained the goddess by endlessly jabbering on. For her role in Zeus' adultery, Hera punished Echo by impoverishing her ability to speak. From then on Echo could not say anything of her own, she could only repeat the words of others. So when Narcissus heard a twig snap and called out, 'Is there anyone here?' she could not cry, 'Yes!' but only, 'Here!'

'Why won't you come to me?' Narcissus asked.

'Come to me!' Echo replied.

'Where are you?'

'Where are you?'

'Don't hide, let us meet.'

'Let us meet!' Echo said, and emerged from the thicket, approaching Narcissus with open arms, but he recoiled.

'Stay away,' he said. 'I don't want your hands on me.'

'Your hands on me …' she repeated, and shrank away in shame, back into the woods, seeking solace in the company of caves. The rejection destroyed her; her body shrivelled with grief. Her skin dried to dust and scattered in the passing wind. Her bones cast off their wasted muscle and turned to stone. All that remained of her was a voice, a lonely sound that continues to be heard in valleys and gullies; the empty spaces where she remains living.

Narcissus would come to experience the suffering he had caused in others. One of those he had scorned lifted his hands to the sky and said, 'Let him know this pain. Teach him how it hurts.' Nemesis heard the plea and granted it.

It was a sultry day when Narcissus fell in love with his own reflection. Bending down to scoop water from a lake, he felt his stomach flutter at the sudden sight of the beauty staring back at him. He was bewitched by those large dark eyes, which were his, those strong curling locks, which were his, and those soft flushed cheeks, which were his. He was besotted; he couldn't take his eyes off himself. He reached his arms into the water to try and touch his lover, but the image fragmented into ripples and vanished.

The weight of desire was torturous. Narcissus was convinced that his feelings were requited because as he leaned in to kiss the water, the other, himself, also lifted his face closer. They had a connection, a perfect harmony of action and understanding. And though he soon came to realise that the person was himself reflected, it did nothing to temper his feelings. His desire would not subside, nor would his pain. There was nothing in the world more beautiful than his reflection, this untouchable body of water and light.

Defeated by the impossibility of his love, Narcissus eventually weakened and died. As he fell he shed a single tear at the thought that his beloved would not outlive him.

Hermeneutic Question 3   Does this story have a moral? If so, do you accept the moral?

Task Question 2   Is self-love bad?

Questions to take you further

- Can self-love be satisfied? Can it be requited? Is it enough?
- Is self-love an obstacle to love of others?
- Is self-love necessary for a good life?
- Is selfishness at the root of all bad?
- Is selflessness at the root of all good?
- Is identifying with another person a poor basis for loving them?
- Is humility a virtue?

❖ Is morality based on sacrifice?

❖ Should we prioritise our desires over others'?

❖ When you love yourself, what is it you love?

Lying

Truth is entirely and absolutely a matter of style.

Oscar Wilde

Starter Question 1   If you tell a lie in a forest and no one is around to hear it, is it a lie?

Starter Question 2   What is a lie?

Questions to take you further

❖ Can you lie to yourself?

❖ Is something a lie even if the speaker believes it is true?

❖ Is something a lie even if the speaker wishes it were true?

❖ Is an exaggeration a lie?

❖ Is something a lie even if the listener isn't interested in being told the truth?

❖ Can a lie be true?

Oscar Wilde speculated on the birth of lies. He believed it all started with not wanting to get out of bed.

Wilde imagined a caveman with a lively mind and tired body. One morning he decided not to go out on the hunt; instead, he stayed in bed and envisioned it. When the sun set that evening and the other cavemen returned to huddle round the fire, he stood before them and recounted his day, vividly describing his heroic conquests. He spoke of the mammoth he had slain, of his strength and fearlessness before the beast. His fellow cavemen were captivated by the story, though, of course, not a word of it was true.

Wilde applauded this invented inventor of lies. He said that the wish of the liar is simply, 'to charm, to delight, to give pleasure'.

Others have shared Wilde's enthusiasm for lies, though their passion has tended to be rather less positive. Here are some remarks plucked from time:

'No happiness can be yours if the Lie-demon drives the chariot of your lives.' Zarathustra, Gathas

'A righteous man hates lying.' Proverbs 13:5

'Do not mix truth with falsehood, or hide the truth when you know it.' Qur'an 2:42

'Putrid fever makes them reek with a stench.' The suffering of liars in the Eighth Circle of Hell, Dante's *Inferno*

'Lying is *mean* and makes a human being unworthy of happiness.' Immanuel Kant, *The Metaphysics of Morals*

'Abhor dishonesty, any kind of dishonesty, but above all, dishonesty with regard to your own self.' Fyodor Dostoyevsky, *The Brothers Karamazov*

Hermeneutic Question   Why is lying thought to be wrong?

Questions to take you further

❖ Why do we value truth?

❖ Why do we value knowledge?

❖ Is fantasy ever more important than reality?

❖ Is the imagination a compulsive liar?

❖ Is the hatred of lying a hatred of the imagination?

❖ Why would anyone hate the imagination?

❖ Is the purpose of speech to exchange truths?

❖ 'The truth will set you free', John 8:32. Is there a relation between truth and freedom?

In 2007 a man in America named Xavier Alvarez was sent to court for telling a lie. One day Alvarez boasted to his colleagues that he had been awarded the Medal of Honor – the highest military honour in the US – after being wounded in action as a marine.

Alvarez hadn't in fact been given this award; he hadn't even served in the armed forces. A colleague of his knew this and reported Alvarez to the authorities. Under the Stolen Valor Act 2005, it was illegal in the US to lie about having received US military decoration.

Alvarez was sentenced to pay a $5,000 fine, but he appealed and the case went to the Supreme Court. There it was decided that the law should be changed and Alvarez' charges were cleared. The Supreme Court argued that a law against lying violates the First Amendment of the US Constitution, which grants all citizens the right to free speech.

Task Question 1   Should lying be a crime?

Questions to take you further

❖ If it is wrong, should it be illegal?

❖ Are all wrong actions harmful?

❖ Should all harmful actions be illegal?

❖ Should all actions worthy of punishment be illegal?

❖ Is lying harmful?

❖ Would a law against lying make society more trustworthy?

❖ Should the law be used to make us better people?

❖ Should we have the right to free speech?

❖ Does the right to free speech value freedom over truth?

It may be said that lying ought to be illegal in those instances in which it has bad consequences (a miscarriage of justice, a war, etc.). However, it's not clear that the problem here is with lying or just acting with malice, so it would be worth enquiring whether telling a truth that we know will cause damage is equally blameworthy. The answer may contain within it the view that lies are inherently destructive (or that truth is inherently good). If so, it would be good to explore the reasons for believing this.

Present the following argument:

1.   Truth is good.

2.   Lying is wrong because it hides the truth.

3.   Secrets also hide the truth.

4.   Therefore, secrets are like lies.

5.   Therefore, it is wrong to keep secrets.

Task Question 2   Is this a good argument?

The bullet point questions for this Task Question will simply address the goodness of the premises. Approach the Task Question by first asking for hands on who accepts the conclusion. Explain that if they don't accept the conclusion they will need to reject one of the premises (see Appendix 6), and go through the argument one premise at a time, discussing their reasons for either accepting or rejecting them.

Torture

The word is the shadow of the deed.

Democritus

In 2002 a law student in Germany kidnapped the 11-year-old son of a wealthy banker. The man, Magnus Gäfgen, contacted the boy's father and said that he would return the boy in exchange for €1,000,000. When Gäfgen went to collect the money he was arrested, but the boy remained missing.

In order to establish the boy's whereabouts, the kidnapper was interrogated by the police for many hours, but he would not cooperate. Fearing the boy was in danger, possibly dying, the police became desperate. The deputy chief considered the illegal option of torture. He ordered a colleague to enter the interrogation room and threaten the kidnapper. They told Gäfgen that if he did not reveal the location of the boy, they would torture him until he did. They warned that a torture specialist had been sent for.

Though torture, and the threat of it, is illegal, the police believed it was a necessary step. The idea of inflicting a momentary, albeit severe, level of pain in order to secure a lasting good may seem wholly practical.

However, this characterisation of torture conflicts with the comment made by the Jewish writer, Jean Améry, that 'whoever was tortured, stays tortured'.

Améry was a Jew who fled Austria at the dawn of the Second World War and joined the resistance in Belgium, where he was captured and tortured by the Gestapo. Years after the war he wrote of his experience: 'Frail in the face of violence, yelling out in pain, awaiting no help, capable of no resistance, the tortured person is only a body, and nothing else beside that ... Torture is the most horrible event a human being can retain within himself ... Whoever has succumbed to torture can no longer feel at home in the world ... It is *fear* that henceforth reigns over him ... if worst comes to worst, he is driven beyond the border of death into Nothingness.'

Task Question 1 Would it have been wrong of the police to torture the man?

Questions to take you further

* Is torture absolutely wrong?

* Is it a matter of weighing up the costs and consequences?

* Is it sometimes a necessary evil? Or is the idea of necessary evil itself evil?

* Would it be wrong to force someone to act as the torturer?

* Would it be better if there were professionals, people who tortured for a living? Would such a job pose any risks to the workers?

(Once threatened Gäfgen did disclose the location of the boy, but he was already dead. Gäfgen was sentenced to life imprisonment. He was given €3,000 in damages for his treatment by the police. The deputy chief police officer was charged €10,800.)

In the Old Testament there is a verse that has been interpreted as a prohibition against torture. It reads:

Remember them that are in bonds, as bound with them; and them which suffer adversity, as being yourselves also in the body. (Hebrews 13:3)

Hermeneutic Question What does this mean? Is it true?

Questions to take you further

- Are we of the same body as other people?
- Are we separate from other people?
- Is there such a thing as a total stranger?
- When we hurt other people, are we also hurting ourselves?
- If the verse is true, why do we forget it?

The 18th century Scottish philosopher Adam Smith believed that sympathy was essential to morality. He thought that our desire to do good comes from our capacity to sympathise with others. He wrote:

By the imagination we place ourselves in his situation, we conceive ourselves enduring all the same torments, we enter as it were into his body, and become in some measure the same person with him, and thence form some idea of his sensations. His agonies, when they are thus brought home to ourselves, when we have thus adopted and made them our own, begin at last to affect us, and we then tremble and shudder at the thought of what he feels. This is the source of our fellow feeling for the misery of others, by changing places in fancy with the sufferer.

Our ability to imagine the experiences of others is what compels us to help them. But in the case of torture this is precisely what the torturer cannot do. The torturer is not at liberty to imagine themselves in the position of their victim. In order to inflict pain, the torturer must forgo sympathy.

Task Question 2   Do all people deserve sympathy?

Questions to take you further

❖ Do you agree with Smith that when we sympathise with others we enter into their bodies and become the same person?

❖ Are there people it would be wrong to become the same person with?

❖ Is sympathy compatible with war?

❖ Could sympathy ever get in the way of us doing the right thing?

❖ Is it possible to punish sympathetically?

❖ Are there people it is impossible to sympathise with?

❖ Is there such a thing as too much kindness?

In 2012 the Oscar-winning director Kathryn Bigelow released a film called *Zero Dark Thirty* about the death of Osama Bin Laden, which featured scenes that depict the torture of al-Qaeda suspects. The film was criticised as obscene because it was perceived to glorify and condone torture.

It has been argued that torture should never be shown on film, whether it's glorified or not. There are certain horrors that should not be touched, that should be excluded from the imagination and considered out of bounds. The South African novelist J. M. Coetzee believes this. He has written:

It is obscene. Obscene because such things ought not to take place, and then obscene again because having taken place they ought not to be brought into the light but covered up and hidden forever in the bowels of the earth. To save our humanity, certain things that we may want to see must remain off-stage. Death is a private matter; the artist should not invade the deaths of others.

Task Question 3   Is it wrong to depict torture?

Questions to take you further

* Are there things we shouldn't know?

* Is it wrong to take pleasure in fictional violence?

* If we are constantly shown suffering, could we become immune to it?

* Can it be good for us to watch suffering?

* Can images harm us? What does Coetzee mean when he speaks of saving our humanity?

* Is a depiction always a lie? (If the depiction were realistic, could we bear to see it?)

* Is all censorship wrong? Should we be free to watch whatever we choose?

* Are taboos sometimes necessary?

* Is it wrong to broadcast or watch footage of real people dying? Should (say) 9/11 videos be removed from the internet?

Other Minds

I think that once you see emotions from a certain angle you can never think of them as real again.

Andy Warhol

Psychologists have documented an unnerving condition they call Capgras Delusion. Those suffering from this condition believe that their friends or family have been replaced by impostors who are the spitting image of them. Sometimes they believe that certain people are robots – they search their bodies looking for wires and switches.

The delusion that other people are robots is bound up with the belief that other people do not really experience feelings or emotions, that behind their eyes is nothing; they lack so-called 'mental states'.

Imagine that you encounter someone suffering from this delusion. The person believes that you are a robot. They are convinced that, unlike a real person, you don't experience feelings or emotions.

Starter Question 1   Could you prove that you really do experience feelings and emotions?

Questions to take you further

* How do we know that other people do?

* If it can't be proved, does that mean it shouldn't be believed? Is it a belief?

* Is it easy to imagine other people as robots?

* When you see a person cry, is their sadness something you've worked out? Are their tears *evidence* of sadness?

Some pupils, with the idea of the robot in mind, may say that you could cut yourself and show that there is blood rather than oil. Return them to the ques-

tion by asking, 'Does having blood prove that we have emotions?' Whatever proof is suggested, you can then direct the class to the first bullet point; for example, if it is suggested that displaying the activity in our brains would constitute proof, you can ask whether it is on this same basis that we know that other people experience emotions, and if not, are we then justified in thinking that they do?

Starter Questions 2   A woman walks into a police station and starts shivering. What might she be going through? What might she be feeling?

Questions to take you further

❖ What more would you need to know about her to fully understand her behaviour?

❖ Is there a limit to our interpretations of what she might be feeling?

❖ What makes an interpretation of other people good or bad?

❖ Do all people behave and react in roughly similar ways?

This question is turning away from whether people feel and experience towards the more ordinary concern of what they feel and experience. It is wondering how we make sense of other people, what we need to know about them if we are to know them. With the shivering woman you can explore a range of possible feelings. If she is feeling cold, are there different kinds of cold? Could it be the cold of fever, or the cold of deep winter, or the cold of dawn, or the cold of exposure? Are there different kinds of nervousness? Different kinds of shudders? Is the woman a criminal or a victim?

Encourage alternatives to proliferate, invite as many variables as possible. The basic wonder is: how precise and exact can your interpretations be? This can be approached by taking a number of different interpretations and asking which is the most likely, and by what criteria this likelihood is assessed. Faced with so many variables and possibilities, how are we ever able to understand other people?

Shakespeare's *King Lear* opens with the elderly patriarch announcing his retirement. He wants to divide Britain among his three daughters, but not in equal measure. He explains that the daughter who shows him, through speech, that they love him the most will receive the greatest share of the land. His first daughter speaks:

Sir, I do love you more than word can wield the matter,
Dearer than eyesight, space and liberty,
Beyond what can be valued, rich or rare,
No less than life, with grace, health, beauty, honour.
As much as child e'er loved, or father found,
A love that makes breath poor and speech unable,
Beyond all manner of so much I love you.

His second daughter follows:

Sir, I am made of that same mettle as my sister,
And prize me at her worth. In my true heart
I find she names my very deed of love:
Only she comes too short, that I profess
Myself an enemy to all other joys
Which the most precious square of sense possesses,
And find I am alone felicitate
In your dear highness' love.

Lear then turns to the third. He tells her to speak. She replies, 'Nothing, my lord.' Lear tells her to try again:

Unhappy that I am, I cannot heave
My heart into my mouth. I love your majesty
According to my bond, no more nor less.

Hermeneutic Question   Which of his three daughters do you think loves Lear the most?

Questions to take you further

❖ Is a test of speech a good test of love?

❖ Is there a better test of love that Lear might give?

❖ Does love require testing?

❖ Is there a test that would prove who truly meant what they said?

❖ Is there a test that would prove the meaning of what they said?

The class may find the language difficult and this is partly the point, to interpret ambiguity. To alleviate the frustrating sense that they don't get it, you can ask them to imagine that, like you, Lear is not familiar with Shakespeare's English (you can also ask them to first try and get the gist of the lines – don't get tangled in particular words, but begin by intuiting the flavour of the passage). Then bring in the fifth bullet point and ask them to consider whether the difficulties of interpreting the words of people they know can be as involved as interpreting Shakespeare's words.

Task Question 1   Is it possible to know for sure what other people are feeling?

Questions to take you further

* Can we test what a person is feeling?

* Do we have to know *why* a person is feeling the way they are to know *what* they are feeling?

* Is interpreting a person like interpreting the words of Lear's daughters?

* Are all our actions open to interpretation?

* Can we know what a person is feeling without having the words to say it? Can we possess knowledge we can't express?

* Are we all fairly easy to understand or are we complicated, even fathomless?

* What is the difference between empathy and sympathy? Which is better?

* Does sympathy require knowledge?

* Is understanding people like understanding atoms? Is it like science?

* What is the difference between interpretation and explanation? Is it possible to explain others?

* Are there experts on human nature?

Lear is furious with the answer of his third daughter, Cordelia. He has heard her words and he thinks he has understood their meaning, he thinks that she has slighted him. He judges her words and he condemns her, disowning her as his daughter. He tells her that she is no longer entitled to either his land or his affection, that she is now a stranger to him.

Task Question 2   Is it possible to judge others?

Questions to take you further

❖ To judge a person do we need to know them?

❖ Could we live without judging others? Is judgement necessary? Is it inevitable?

❖ If God is the best judge of us, what qualifies Him for this?

❖ Is everyone doing the best they can?

❖ Should we punish people for their characters or their actions?

❖ Are a person's actions and their character two separate things?

❖ Was it wrong of Lear to disown Cordelia?

❖ What is judgement? What is its purpose?

Language and Discrimination

'How did you know that it was St Michael?'
'By the way he spoke and his language of angels.'
'How did you know it was the language of angels?'
'I soon believed it was. I wanted to believe that it was.'

Joan of Arc, on trial

Task Question 1   Is language power?

Questions to take you further

❖ Can language change the way we think?

❖ Can language change the way we act?

❖ Can language give us power over others?

- Can language improve the world?

- Can language harm the world? Can words be as damaging as sticks and stones?

- Does increasing your vocabulary increase your power?

- Wittgenstein wrote, 'To imagine a language is to imagine a form of life.' What do you think this means?

This Task Question has no corresponding stimulus and is perhaps, in isolation, a little surprising. This openness allows for a more exploratory approach to the question and for the pupils to find their own interpretation of the question. It gives the class a greater uncertainty as to what they are talking about. You might, for example, discuss the question in relation to the time and thought that parents invest in naming their children; you might also read Genesis 2:18–24 – the original use of language, according to the Bible – as a parable on the power of language, and discuss what, as a parable, it is trying to say.

Starter Question 1   What is meant by the word 'chav'?

There is a question of dialect here. In some schools I've taught in, pupils were not familiar with this word. With the Starter Question and the following passage, you can substitute whatever pejorative word your pupils recognise as connoting poverty.

Talking in a radio interview, the musician Plan B expressed his thoughts on the word:

This is a derogatory term used by certain sectors of Middle England to define people from poor and unfortunate backgrounds that have less money than them, that haven't as good an education. And for me that term is no different from similar terms used to be derogatory towards race and sex – the only difference being that the word 'chav' is used very publicly in the press. If similar terms to do with race or sex was used that publicly in the papers there would be a public outcry, and rightly so.

It is a criminal offence in the UK to verbally assault someone on the basis of their disability, race, religion, sexual orientation and transgender identity. These are known as 'hate crimes'.

Task Question 2   Should the use of this word be classified as a hate crime?

Questions to take you further

❖ Is the word a mere description, like 'Asian', 'Jewish' and 'gay'?

❖ Is the word a legitimate judgement, like 'lazy', 'greedy' and 'cowardly'?

❖ What is the difference between a judgement and a prejudice?

❖ Is the word harmful?

❖ Are we responsible for our class?

❖ Is discrimination ever acceptable?

❖ Do hate crimes violate our right to free speech?

❖ Should the use of the word 'toff' be classified as a hate crime?

Plan B mentioned two categories of discrimination – race and sex – but only one of these is encompassed by hate crime legislation.

Starter Question 2 What derogatory words are there related to sex?

Task Question 3 Should the use of these words be classed as a hate crime?

Questions to take you further

* Are there any acceptable expressions of hatred?

* What should we do with our hatred?

* What does hatred want with language? Why isn't it mute?

* There are books of love poems but not of hate poems. Why is this?

* Why is abuse against certain groups ignored?

Task Question 4 Why do people discriminate?

Questions to take you further

* Why is there a paucity of derogatory terms for wealthy white men?

* Who controls language?

* Homophobic people are not content to refer to gay people as 'gay', racist people do not say 'Pakistani', classist people prefer not to use 'poor' or 'working class'. Why does discrimination require its own language?

* Is discrimination based on fear or ignorance or blind rage or something else?

* Is there a cure for discrimination?

Nature

When I brought Hofmann up to see Pollock … one of the questions he asked Jackson was, 'Do you work from nature?' – as there were no still lives around or models around – and Jackson's answer was, 'I am nature.'

Lee Krasner

Starter Question 1   What is nature?

Questions to take you further

❖ Are humans natural? Are we manmade?

❖ Is Mumbai as natural as the Nile? Is an email as natural as a storm?

❖ Are humans the only creatures that can violate nature?

❖ Is terrorism natural?

❖ Are numbers part of nature?

❖ Is the afterlife part of nature?

❖ Is a spider's web natural? Is a beaver's dam natural?

❖ Is anything more natural than anything else?

I leave the house and take a walk. This is what I do:

1.   I pluck a leaf.

2.   I break a branch.

3.   I chop down a tree.

4.   I burn down a forest.

5.   I flood a continent.

6.   I freeze the Earth.

Starter Question 2 At which point do my actions become wrong, if at all?

With a slippery slope such as this, you're questioning how it is possible to stop at any particular point, looking for where the qualitative shift lies. If you think my actions become wrong at 3, what is the qualitative difference between this and 2? The idea is to establish the pupils' ethical attitudes towards the environment. Pupils may say that there are circumstances under which all the actions would be permissible, even right. In order to address their basic attitudes towards nature, it should also be asked whether, and at which stage, the actions are wrong when they are done simply for the hell of it.

Task Question 1 Do trees have rights?

Questions to take you further

❖ Does nature have value in itself?

❖ Are all living things sacred?

❖ Do only sentient things have rights?

❖ Do some things have more rights than others?

❖ If trees don't have rights, are there other reasons why it might be wrong to damage them?

❖ Is chopping down a tree murder?

Smallpox existed for at least 3,000 years. Its rash has been found on the faces of Egyptian mummies. In the 20th century alone, an estimated 300 million people died from it. It is a disease caused by the variola virus; its most conspicuous symptom is blistering which develops all over the body, even in the mouth and throat, but mostly on the face and arms. It kills approximately a third of all those infected.

Though there is no cure, smallpox was officially eradicated in 1979. The variola virus, however, still exists. It is preserved in two high-security facilities, one in Russia and the other in the US. The World Health

Organization (WHO), which was instrumental in its eradication, has been calling for its complete destruction for decades.

The request by the WHO has raised concern. It has been argued that if the virus were to be destroyed, it would be the first instance of humans intentionally acting with the explicit goal of eliminating another life form from the planet. It would constitute an unthinking disregard for nature. In arguing for the conservation of species, the biologist David Ehrenfeld has said, 'they should be conserved because they exist and because this existence is itself but the present expression of a continuing historical process of immense antiquity and majesty'.

The deliberate extinction of a species – the total annihilation of a life form – is perhaps an act worthy of moral scrutiny.

Task Question 2   Does the variola virus have rights?

Questions to take you further

❖ Should it be made extinct?

❖ Does it deserve extinction?

❖ Are rights based on desert? Do harmful things not deserve rights?

❖ Do we have the right to deliberately make a species extinct?

❖ Should we be humbled by nature? Is it greater than us? Is it majestic?

❖ Is all life intrinsically valuable?

❖ A virus is unable to move, grow or reproduce without first inhabiting a living cell. Is a virus a living thing?

The Earth's history has been characterised by environmental volatility. It has passed through periods of extinction and vast climatic change. There have been times when the Earth was a blazing desert and times when it was mostly ice.

Around 850 million years ago, during the Cryogenian period, the Earth was a snowball. It is hypothesised that the cold was so severe that the ice stretched all the way to the equator. At this point life consisted only of tiny organisms. Then, as the Earth underwent a period of extreme global warming, the ice melted, and 500 million years later, towards the end of the Devonian period, forests and animals were populating the land for the first time in Earth's history. But mass extinction followed and three quarters of all life died out, possibly due to global cooling.

When life returned it brought with it the Earth's first mighty carnivore, Dinogorgon, but that too would disappear during what is called 'the Great Dying', a period in which 96% of species died out. This is the most severe mass extinction the Earth has yet seen.

Fast forward 100 million years and the dinosaurs are thriving. They exist in abundance, a great diversity of shapes and sizes. But, of course, they will also be wiped out. Their decline is thought to have started with immense volcanic eruptions that affected the climate, and concluded with an asteroid or comet crashing into the Earth.

Now, 65 million years later, here we are.

Task Question 3   Is global warming the destruction of nature or just an ordinary stage in its tumultuous history?

Questions to take you further

* Is global warming bad for nature?

* Can nature be a victim? Can nature be destroyed?

* Is global warming something we are doing to nature or something nature is doing to us?

* Is there a thing – a kind of being or force – called nature? Or is nature just the sum of all natural things?

❖ Is it selfish of us to want to preserve the world as it currently is, to preserve the conditions that sustain our species?

❖ Should we mind whether future humans become extinct or not?

❖ Do we have duties towards future people?

Temptation

For a pure sense of being tumultuously alive, you can't beat the nasty side of existence.

Philip Roth

In Plato's *The Republic,* Socrates makes the observation that bad characters are dramatically more interesting than good characters.

Think about plays, novels or films you like.

Starter Question   Are the good or the bad characters the most interesting? Why is this?

There is apparently something alluring about being bad. In the story of Adam and Eve, a story which is thought to document our true and original nature, humans are presented as creatures that have an incurable fascination with the bad. We can't help but want what we shouldn't.

In the myth of the Fall, the bad is concentrated in the forbidden fruit. Though we are commanded not to eat the fruit, it is, as Milton writes in *Paradise Lost,* fair to the eye, ruddy and gold, possessed of a sweet smell, inviting to the taste, exhilarating in prospect. It proves too tempting for Eve and her longing eye gets the better of her. She takes a bite and the taste is more delightful than any fruit she has ever eaten. The pleasure of the badness is so intense she wishes there were more she shouldn't do.

The idea that badness offers pleasure reverberates in the legend of Faust. Faust was apparently a real person, a scholar of medicine and magic, who lived in Germany in the 16th century, and sold his soul to the devil, an act for which he was hounded out of town.

According to the legend, Faust enters into a contract with the ministers of hell, using his blood to sign on the dotted line. In exchange for his soul, the devil, or one of his agents, will serve Faust for 24 years, giving him whatever he wants, obeying his will and whim, letting him live in all voluptuousness. Over the years Faust uses his demonic licence to acquire knowledge, explore the world, gorge on pearls and gold, listen to the recitations of Homer, steal food from under the Pope's nose, become a great musician and get romantic with Helen of Troy.

The story suggests that by giving up our soul, the origin of our goodness, we can experience all manner of enjoyment; if only we abjured our devotion to the good, we could lead wonderfully pleasurable lives. As Lucifer says in Marlowe's *Doctor Faustus*, 'In hell is all manner of delight'; as Mephistopheles says of Goethe's Faust, 'He shall eat dust and do so with delight.' Maybe the bad are having all the fun.

Task Question 1   Is it more pleasurable to be bad or good?

Questions to take you further

❖ Is it pleasurable to be good?

❖ Is it pleasurable to be bad? Are the bad having all the fun?

❖ Who has greater freedom: the good or the bad?

❖ What is goodness? Why do we want it? Why don't we want it?

❖ What is badness? Why do we want it? Why don't we want it?

❖ Is there such a thing as too much pleasure?

The idea of temptation suggests an internal battle between good and bad, a conflict of desires. This dualism of good and bad can be found in the ancient Persian religion, Zoroastrianism. Zoroastrianism speaks of life as a choice between two opposing forces: Ahura Mazda, the creator of life and goodness, and Angra Mainyu, a destructive and evil energy. The religion is founded on the teachings of Zarathustra, who in his hymns, the Gathas, said:

In the beginning there were two primal spirits, Twins spontan-
eously active;
These are the Good and the Evil, in thought, and in word, and in
deed:
Between these two, let the wise choose aright;
Be good, not base.
The worst existence shall be the lot of the followers of evil.
And the good mind shall be the reward of the followers of good.

This conflict is often portrayed in cartoons with an angel on one shoulder and a devil on the other. Zarathustra thought the choice was easy. His religion is an optimistic one; he is said to have been the only baby who was not born crying but laughing.

Task Question 2   Is life a war between good and bad?

Questions to take you further

* Was the Second World War a battle of good vs. bad?

* Are some people good and others bad?

* Are good and bad opposites?

* Is 'criminal' our name for those who are losing the war?

* Is the war an easy one?

* Do good and bad really exist?

In Marlowe's play, the Good Angel tells Faustus that contrition, prayer and repentance will lead him to heaven, but the Bad Angel says that these are illusions. One of the perceived pleasures of signing away our souls and severing the connection to the good is the consequent freedom from guilt.

Guilt, claimed the 19th century philosopher Friedrich Nietzsche, is a form of self-harm; it is aggression turned inwards. We attack ourselves with an unremitting belief in our own unworthiness, with self-accusation and biting self-judgement. And we do this in order to sustain our search for forgiveness and redemption.

Guilt gives life meaning, it gives us a purpose and direction, a longing to be decent and worthy. To ensure we never satisfy our goal of being good, we place impossible standards on ourselves; the worse we feel the more meaning we have. Though guilt has a purpose, Nietzsche was adamant that it is poisonous, an aversion to life, wretched self-denial, a saboteur.

Task Question 3   Is guilt bad?

Questions to take you further

❖ Is guilt a cruel burden? Is it a consequence of impossible standards?

❖ Is guilt an appropriate punishment?

❖ Should those who do wrong feel guilty? Should we try to make them feel guilty?

❖ Do we need guilt to be good?

❖ Is there such a thing as too much guilt?

❖ Can you imagine living a guilt-free life?

❖ Does guilt have a purpose?

❖ Why do we feel it?

Sin

I feel I must … atone – is that the word?

T. S. Eliot

In the 6th century, Pope Gregory the Great outlined what have become known as the 'seven deadly sins'. The list has changed over the years, but this is how it currently stands in the *Catechism of the Catholic Church*:

❖ Pride

❖ Lust

❖ Avarice

❖ Envy

- ❖ Gluttony
- ❖ Wrath
- ❖ Sloth

Writing in *Moralia on Job*, Gregory the Great claimed that pride is foundational, the beginning of all sin. Each of his listed sins proliferate and fission, which is why they are also called 'capital', as well as 'deadly'. Wrath leads to strife, insults and blasphemy. From gluttony arises 'foolish mirth', uncleanness, babbling and dullness in understanding. From lust comes 'blindness of mind', inconstancy, impetuosity and self-love. Envy engenders hatred and sadism. Avarice creates deceit, restlessness, violence and a hardness of the heart.

Each sin runs into the other and gives rise to more.

Starter Question   How would you list the vices in terms of severity?

Questions to take you further

- ❖ Would you add anything to the list?
- ❖ Would you remove anything from the list?

Task Question 1   Are they sins?

Questions to take you further

- ❖ If they are not sins, what are they?
- ❖ Are they bad for our health? Is avoiding them a lifestyle choice?
- ❖ Are they truly terrible, truly destructive?
- ❖ Are they harmful? What in us do they harm? How do they harm?
- ❖ Why would we harm ourselves?
- ❖ Do we really behave like this? Or is it made up?

❖ What is sin? Is there a difference between calling something wrong and calling it a sin?

❖ Do we need the idea of sin?

Inverting the vices, you can additionally ask the class to draw up a list of perfections, a list of what they believe to be the seven supreme virtues, the seven attributes and characteristics that they admire and aspire to. Taking an assorted seven from different pupils, you can then open it up for discussion: 'Do you accept this list? Would you like to be a person with these virtues?' You might consider, say, whether humility is a virtue, or thriftiness, or politeness, loyalty, patriotism, obedience, defiance, daring, shamelessness, self-belief, silliness, strength, weakness, intelligence, passion, curiosity, trust, doubt, etc. One way to arrive at some candidate virtues is to wonder what the opposite of each sin is.

In defining sin, philosophers and theologians have emphasised its conceptual relation to God. They have written:

Aquinas, 13th century: 'The guilty character of sin consists in the fact that it is committed against God.'

Kant, 18th century: sin means 'trespass of the moral law as divine command'.

Kierkegaard, 19th century: 'Human guilt becomes sin when the guilty person knows he stands before God'.

Nicolai Hartmann, 20th century: sin is 'the same moral guilt of which ethics also speaks, but not "as" moral guilt, that is, not as guilt before the forum of one's own conscience and its values, but rather as guilt *before God*'.

Task Questions 2

- Can you believe in sin without believing in God?
- Is there any point in believing in sin if you don't believe in God?
- Can you believe in God without believing in sin?
- If sin is not a betrayal of God, what is it a betrayal of?
- Is the word 'sin' an important part of our moral vocabulary? Could we do without it?
- If God isn't the foundation of morality, what is? Where does our conscience come from?
- What do you need to believe in to believe in sin?

Feelings and Rights

Majesty and love go ill together.

Ovid

Consider these reasons why we shouldn't bully others:

1. It violates their rights.
2. It is unkind.
3. It is against school rules.

Starter Question How would you rank the reasons in terms of importance?

Questions to take you further

- Is one reason enough?
- Are the reasons each very different or do they overlap?
- Is there an important reason that is not on the list?

Imagine a great disagreement breaking out over the reasons for why we ought to be moral. The two opposing sides feel that they simply can't communicate with each other; they can't make sense of each other's words, they are bewildered by the other point of view. Eventually, and amicably, they decide to divide the world in two. Half the world is going to become the Half of Rights while the other will be the Half of Feelings.

In the Half of Rights they never speak about feelings and in the Half of Feelings they never speak about rights. The Half of Rights believes it is wrong to humiliate others because it violates their right to be treated with respect. The Half of Feelings says that humiliation is wrong because it leads to hurt and suffering.

In the Half of Rights they believe that the best we can do for other people is to respect them. But in the Half of Feelings there is no such word as 'respect'. They believe that the best we can do for others is to be kind to them. They speak of 'sympathy' instead of 'respect'. The Half of Rights believes sympathy is irrelevant. We only need to follow our duty.

In the Half of Rights they have no such word as 'cruelty'. They think that the worst thing we do to other people is rob them of their dignity, undermine their sense of autonomous individuality. The Half of Feelings does not know the word 'dignity'. They think the worst thing we do to other people is turn our backs on them, turn them out into the cold and harden our hearts towards them.

It is widely believed in the Half of Rights that one must be prepared to fight. Rights are things we need to protect and sometimes they need to be fought for. The Half of Feelings wouldn't want to say that anything that leads to violence is necessary, even if it is unavoidable. They wouldn't wish to enshrine this. They widely believe that though we must sometimes be able to ask for kindness and help, this cannot be forced.

In the Half of Rights it is believed that what is most significant about us is our capacity to think and act for ourselves, and that what we need more of is the space in which to do this. In the Half of Feelings it is believed that what is most significant about us is our helplessness, and that help is what we need more of.

Both halves believe in equality. For the Half of Rights we are all equally entitled. For the Half of Feelings we are all equal in need.

Board the respective moral vocabularies of the two halves:

Words commonly used in the Half of Rights	Words commonly used in the Half of Feelings
respect	sympathy
dignity	cruelty
autonomy	coldness
individuality	solidarity
entitlement	helplessness
duty	need
protection	kindness

Task Question 1   Which would be the better half?

Questions to take you further

❖ Would the two halves be different?

❖ Are the two halves incompatible?

❖ Is dignity compatible with helplessness?

❖ Is kindness compatible with individuality?

❖ Can we get by without respect?

❖ What is more important: sympathy or respect?

In 1948 the member states of the newly formed United Nations adopted the Universal Declaration of Human Rights as 'a common standard of achievement for all peoples and all nations'. It outlines the rights to which all people are entitled. Here are several of its statements:

The recognition of the inherent dignity and of the equal and inalienable rights of all members of the human family is the foundation of freedom, justice and peace in the world.

All human beings are born free and equal in dignity and rights. They are endowed with reason and conscience and should act towards one another in a spirit of brotherhood.

Everyone has the right to life, liberty and security of person.

No one shall be subjected to torture or to cruel, inhuman or degrading treatment or punishment.

Everyone has the right to own property.

Everyone has the right to freedom of opinion and expression; this right includes freedom to hold opinions without interference and to seek, receive and impart information and ideas through any media.

The family is the natural and fundamental group unit of society and is entitled to protection by society and the State.

Everyone has the right to rest and leisure.

Elementary education shall be compulsory. Education shall be directed to the full development of the human personality and to the strengthening of respect for human rights and fundamental freedoms.

Hermeneutic Question   Is there anything you disagree with?

Questions to take you further

* What does 'human family' mean?

* What does 'inhuman' mean?

* What does 'human personality' mean?

* Is our being 'endowed with reason' relevant to our moral value?

* Is there anything the Half of Feelings would disagree with?

* How would the Half of Feelings rewrite the declaration?

Task Question 2   Do we need to believe in rights?

Questions to take you further

* Can you be a good person only if you believe that other people have rights?

* Could a sympathetic person who had never heard of rights be a good person?

* Does morality require rules? Is it a matter of playing by the rules?

* Can rules prevent cruelty?

* What is the worst thing about cruelty? That it breaks the rules?

* How can bad people be made good? Would teaching them about rights make them good?

* Is there a difference between saying, 'I *want* to be heard,' and, 'I *have a right* to speak'?

* What are rights? Who decides them? How do we know what rights we have?

* Do we need to believe in dignity in order to be good?

* Do babies and animals have 'inherent dignity'?

* Can we believe in equality without believing in rights? What makes us equal, if not rights?

* Is the belief in rights a significant part of your everyday life?

The Senses

Of all the organs of perception, I would say, the eye is the most sun-like.

Plato

Imagine you were deprived of all your senses. Imagine being born this way.

Starter Question 1   What would it be like?

Questions to take you further

* Would you have thoughts?

* Would you be aware of time?

* Would you have a sense of existence?

* Would it be like anything?

* Would you exist?

Starter Question 2   Which of the five senses – touch, taste, smell, sight and sound – gives us the most understanding of the world?

Questions to take you further

* Through which of our senses do we sense ourselves? *Do* we sense ourselves?

- Can you imagine a sixth sense? Is our imagination limited to our experience?

- Could there be more to the world than our senses reveal?

- If you were deprived of all senses but one, which would you want to keep?

- Would you rather see the light of the sun or feel its warmth?

- Which sense gives the most pleasure? Is this the one that gives the most understanding?

- Which sense brings us closest to the world? Which sense gives us most awareness of time?

- Are the senses separate or intermingled?

- What does it mean to understand the world?

With the second bullet point you could look at electroreception – the ability of aquatic animals to sense electric fields – and ask the class to imagine possessing this sense. Are we able to imagine what this would be like? Is a shark's experience of an electric field a private mental event that we don't have access to? Do sensory experiences occur within our minds or are they out in the world?

The penultimate bullet point can be considered through an exploration of your class's synaesthetic capacities. You can begin by asking them to try associating particular colours with different numbers (speak the numbers out loud); ask them to arrange numbers one to ten in the order of a rainbow. Additionally, or alternatively, and somewhat messily, you could ask the class to paint what they hear while listening to (say) Debussy's 'Clair de Lune'. Using instruments or their voices, the class could also try to produce the sounds they associate with different textures or colours. Their responses to these tasks will then constitute your data when discussing the bullet point: can we see with our ears? Are there pictures in sound? If sounds are vibrations in the air, where are the images contained? Are the sounds of textures perceived or imagined? If I can't detach my sense of water – the motion of ripples, the glistening beads of light – from

'Clair de Lune', and if the water is imagined rather than perceived, does that mean I don't actually listen to the music but only imagine it? Where does imagination end and perception begin?

Start with a plain circle.

Add individual features.

Starter Question 3   Which feature is the most effective in turning the circle into a person?

Questions to take you further

- What do the eyes reveal about a person?
- Do the eyes reveal the presence of rationality?
- Do the eyes reveal the presence of emotion?
- Do the eyes reveal the presence of curiosity?
- Do the eyes reveal presence?
- Why do you think firing squads typically blindfold their victims?
- Why do babies enjoy playing peekaboo?
- What is a person?

The ancient Greek story of Oedipus begins with divine sight and ends in darkness.

Laius, the king of Thebes, had a curse on his lineage. His line, the House of Labdacus, was doomed to vanish. Laius consulted an oracle on the possibility of producing descendants. He was told if he had a son, the child would murder him and marry Jocasta, the queen, and boy's mother.

Through misfortune, carelessness, or a collusion of the two, the queen soon gave birth to a boy. In light of the oracle's prophecy Laius and Jocasta arranged for the child to be killed. They ordered a servant to leave their son to the elements on a mountainside.

When the time came to turn his back on the child, the servant couldn't bear it. He left the child with a nearby shepherd and returned to Thebes. The shepherd then passed the infant on to the king and queen of Corinth, who had been unable to have children. They named the boy Oedipus and raised him lovingly.

As Oedipus grew older his peers suspected that he was not the biological child of the king and queen; they saw him as an outsider. Oedipus heard the rumours and consulted an oracle. The oracle did not tell him of his origins, but she did tell him that he would kill his father and marry his mother. Oedipus was horrified by the prophecy and fled Corinth to avoid fulfilling it. He decided on travelling to Thebes.

On the road Oedipus encountered King Laius. The two entered into a skirmish over who should have right of way and in a bout of road rage Oedipus struck Laius and killed him. He was, of course, unaware that the dead man at his feet was his father and the king of Thebes.

He continued to Thebes where he found that the Sphinx – a creature half-woman, half-lion, with the wings of an eagle – was terrorising the city. She got her kicks from challenging young Theban men to riddles.

When they failed to crack the riddles, which was always the way, she ate them.

The Thebans begged Oedipus to face the Sphinx. If he could solve her riddle and rid the city of her presence, they would reward him with the city's throne and their queen, Jocasta, his mother. Oedipus rose to the occasion; standing before the Sphinx, poised between tragedy and death, he was asked, 'What singular creature has one voice, one nature, yet goes on two feet, three feet and four feet?' Oedipus answered, 'Humans – when they are young they crawl on all fours, they grow to stand upright and when they are old they use a stick for support.' Upon hearing the correct answer the Sphinx died. Oedipus was crowned king of Thebes and he took Jocasta for his wife. They went on to have four children together.

Years later Thebes was struck by a plague and the oracle was consulted to ascertain its cause. She explained that the plague would not pass till the murderer of Laius was apprehended and banished. While Oedipus was investigating the murder, off in search of himself, a traveller from Corinth arrived to inform him that the king and queen had died. Oedipus was both upset and relieved: if they were dead, there was no chance of the prophecy coming true. 'But,' the traveller went on to say, 'do not be too saddened. They were not really your parents.' Oedipus asked how he could know this. The traveller, it transpired, was the shepherd who had delivered the baby to the royal couple all those years ago.

Jocasta overheard the shepherd's tale and withdrew. She sensed its strange familiarity and she felt sick with inevitability. Her suicide came minutes later.

Oedipus asked the shepherd how the baby came into his possession. The shepherd pointed to the tender-hearted servant, the one who had been entrusted with young Oedipus' death. Oedipus asked the servant who had given him the baby.

'Jocasta,' he said, and the penny dropped.

Oedipus saw how a tangled path had delivered him to his simple fate: he had killed his father and married his mother. Floundering and panicked, Oedipus stabbed out his eyes, blinding himself permanently. Speckled darkness swirled round him, rolling in waves, and he sank to the bottom of the earth as life rose up beyond him; the depths clamped down like bars.

Asked why he had mutilated himself, Oedipus replied, 'What good were eyes to me?'

He exiled himself from Thebes and left without his children – his siblings – who had to be torn from his hands. The rest of his days were occluded by night, unmoored, obscured from light.

Hermeneutic Question   Why did Oedipus blind himself when he discovered the truth?

Questions to take you further

❖ What was Oedipus trying to accomplish?

❖ Is his blindness an attempt to punish or to help himself?

❖ Why, as he implies, were eyes no good to him?

❖ Does he hate his eyes? Or is it the eyes of others that he hates?

❖ Why did he damage his sight and not his other senses? Why not chop off his ears?

❖ In Sophocles' play Oedipus consults the blind prophet, Tiresias (Athena blinded him after he spotted her bathing). Why do you think blindness was thought to contribute to his foreknowledge?

Pointing Exercise:

a.   Point to your nose.

b.   Point to your feet.

c.   Point to your elbow.

d.   Point to your belly button.

e.   Point to your point.

f.   Point to yourself.

Where did you point?

Task Question 1   Why did you/did you not point to your eyes?

Questions to take you further

❖   When we say, 'Look at me,' we mean look at our eyes. Does this mean that our eyes are the location of our selves?

❖   Why do we speak of looking *at* the sky but *into* someone's eyes?

❖   Are eyes the windows to the soul?

❖   Why aren't nostrils the windows to the soul?

❖   Does everything with eyes have a soul?

❖   Why is it rude not to look people in the eyes?

❖   Why can't we fall asleep with our eyes open?

It's nice to repeat the pointing exercise after the discussion to see if, and how, the class do it differently.

Appendices

Appendix 1
Logic dialogue #1

A father said to his son, 'Son, listen to me, I have something very important to tell you: you must never trust anyone or anything.'

'Why?' the boy asked.

'Because people are usually lying or mistaken. The opposite of what they say is more likely to be true,' said the father.

'What about you? Should I trust you?'

'No, you can't even trust me.'

'So is the opposite of what you say more likely to be true?' questioned the boy.

'Yes, that's right.'

'But you said I shouldn't trust anyone. Does that mean I should actually trust everyone?'

'Yes, that's right,' nodded the father.

'And since you say that's right, does that mean it may be wrong?'

'Indeed.'

'Which means I shouldn't actually trust anyone?'

'Certainly! You must never trust anyone.'

'And can I trust you when you tell me this?' the boy asked.

'No, no – you mustn't,' said the father.

'And since you say I mustn't, does that mean I must?'

'You've understood me perfectly, my boy.'

Appendix 2
Logic dialogue #2

A woman is on trial for the alleged murder of her husband.

Barrister Where were you the night of your husband's murder?

Defendant I was staying at my sister's in Bristol.

Barrister Had you spent the day there?

Defendant No, I arrived late afternoon.

Barrister From your home in Cuddesdon?

Defendant Yes.

Barrister At approximately what time?

Defendant About 4.30.

Barrister How long is it in the car from Cuddesdon to Bristol? About an hour and a half?

Defendant About that.

Barrister So you must have left your house at about 3?

Defendant Yes.

Barrister And you are a doctor, is that right?

Defendant Yes.

Barrister So this was a Sunday. Did you not have work the next day in Oxford?

Defendant Yes, I did.

Barrister Why then were you staying at your sister's all the way in Bristol? That's rather a long commute.

Defendant My husband and I had had an argument. I didn't want to be there.

Barrister The last time you saw your husband alive was after an argument?

Defendant Yes.

Barrister Were you angry?

Defendant Yes.

Barrister And then you drove to your sister's in Bristol?

Defendant Yes.

Barrister It was snowing that day, wasn't it?

Defendant Yes.

Barrister What's it like to drive through Cuddesdon in the snow?

Defendant Not easy.

Barrister How much snow fell that day?

Defendant Maybe two feet.

Barrister Those conditions must have been almost impossible.

Defendant Yes.

Barrister So you're feeling emotional, there's two feet of snow – how did you manage to get to your sister's in the ordinary hour and a half?

Defendant I left before it got heavy.

Barrister Did you not just say that there was two feet of snow?

Defendant Yes, but I didn't mean in Cuddesdon. That was how much there was at my sister's.

Barrister Right, and you arrived there at about 4.30.

Defendant Yes, well I think so. Maybe it was closer to 5.30.

Barrister It must have been getting very dark by then.

Defendant Yes.

Barrister Is it true that the week before your husband's murder you received a ticket because your headlights weren't working?

Defendant ... yes, that's correct.

Barrister Had they been repaired by the time of your journey to Bristol?

Defendant ... no.

Barrister Am I right in thinking, then, that you drove to your sister's house in a state of emotional distress, through the snow and in the dark, without the use of your headlights?

Defendant I must have left earlier than that, before it got dark. It was probably closer to 2.

Barrister Did you not just tell the court that you left at 3?

Defendant Yes.

Barrister You left at 2 and you also left at 3. So it would follow then that at 2.30 you were both in Cuddesdon and not in Cuddesdon at the same time. Is that right?

Defendant I'm not sure.

Barrister Where were you the night of your husband's murder?

Defendant I was staying at my sister's in Bristol.

Barrister Had you spent the day there?

Defendant No, I arrived late afternoon.

Barrister From your home in Cuddesdon?

Defendant Yes.

Barrister Why were you staying with her?

Defendant My husband and I had had a fight.

Barrister What about?

Defendant For the past few months he had been talking about moving, living abroad. I didn't want to.

Barrister What sort of man was your husband?

Defendant He was difficult.

Barrister In what way was he difficult?

Defendant He was stubborn, proud; ashamed.

Barrister What was he ashamed of?

Defendant I don't know.

Barrister Was your husband an alcoholic?

Defendant No, but he drank.

Barrister Did he drink too much?

Defendant Yes.

Barrister What do you mean by too much?

Defendant He would just get argumentative. He had a short temper. He wouldn't stop once he got started.

Barrister What would he argue about?

Defendant He blamed me for lots of things. For not being as successful as I could be, for not appreciating him.

Barrister Did you love your husband?

Defendant Yes.

Barrister You loved your husband despite the drinking and the anger and the attacks on your character.

Defendant …

Barrister Were he and your sister on good terms?

Defendant No.

Barrister Why not?

Defendant She never really trusted him.

Barrister Was there a money issue between them?

Defendant … yes.

Barrister What happened?

Defendant She owned a business, a small film production company. The company wasn't doing well. She needed to borrow some money. I didn't have enough and my husband refused to help.

Barrister What happened to the company?

Defendant It was liquidated.

Barrister How did you feel towards your husband for letting that happen?

Defendant I hated him for it.

Barrister You hated your husband?

Defendant Yes.

Barrister Did you ever hate him when he drank and argued?

Defendant I always hated him.

Barrister You always hated your husband?

Defendant Yes.

Barrister But did you not just tell the court that you loved him?

Defendant Yes.

Barrister Let's be clear on this. Did you love your husband or did you hate him?

Defendant Both. Both those things.

Barrister You both loved and hated your husband at the same time?

Defendant Yes.

Appendix 3
Street Art dialogue

Policeman You seem sort of slow in the head – don't make a policeman wait. Most of you lot have the good sense not to spray your crap in broad daylight.

Kid The wall bored me. I did you a favour.

Policeman It's vandalism.

Kid What?

Policeman It's vandalism. You deliberately ruined the building.

Kid That's your opinion. I think I did a great job.

Policeman No, it's not my opinion. It's the law. You don't have the right to interfere with other people's property.

Kid Yeah, I know.

Policeman And you did it anyway?

Kid I don't have the right to interfere with other people's property, sure, but that wall isn't someone else's property. It's mine.

Policeman How exactly is it yours? Somebody paid good money for it. It's their house.

Kid You think that wall is the outside of the owner's house, right? It's not. That wall is the inside of our street. I see that wall every day.

Policeman That wall belongs to the house, which belongs to the owner, who now has to pay to get it cleaned. And he'll have to see your ugly scribble every day till he does.

Photocopiable resource from *Provocations: Philosophy for Secondary School* © David Birch, 2014

Kid Those houses are ugly. You know they tore down a half-pipe to build them. Where that guy's kitchen is, with his bar stools and his giant fridge, that's where me and my friends used to pass the time. I didn't ask for these houses. No one did. Who's to say the buildings aren't vandalism?

Policeman Vandalism?! They were approved by the council! They are family homes.

Kid Well, this street is my home. That wall is my home. I don't care if you want to vandalise my city with buildings just so long as I get to give them some colour.

Policeman The city is for families and businesses, it's made by honest people – people who work hard and do the right thing.

Kid Difference is, you want the street to be a prison, I want it to be a gallery. You want walls to be dividing lines, things that lock us out and the owners in. Because it doesn't matter whether we're the ones locked in or out, when there are dividing lines, it's all the same, everyone's locked up.

Policeman You're boring me now, kid.

Kid Art is about replacing stuff you hate with stuff you love. I hated that wall, now I love it. You don't love anything except law and order. I love beauty. And beauty can't stand law and order. You can't control it. All I'm saying is give beauty a chance, you know?

Policeman Kid, your little cartoon isn't beauty. It's not art. It's just some stupid doodle you made up. Art is serious business. It lasts. Like the *Mona Lisa*. It's not something that gets tagged over or left to fade in the sun.

Kid I'm serious about doodling. And I don't really see the difference between me and da Vinci, except that I'm alive.

Appendix 4
Power dialogue

A I've been wondering what sort of people should rule society.

B Do you think the worst people should rule society?

A Well, no, that's a ridiculous idea.

B So should the best people rule society?

A Yes.

B Would criminals be the best people?

A Certainly not.

B Would people who do not know anything about politics be best?

A No, otherwise they wouldn't know what they were doing.

B So the best people should have studied politics?

A Yes, that seems right.

B Does it follow, then, that the best people should have studied politics at the best places?

A Yes, it does follow.

B And would the best people be those whose opinions aren't clouded by their own personal experiences?

A I should think so. Then they will be fair.

B And isn't it true that the poorest people in society are often the most resentful?

A Yes, you see that.

B So are the poorest people the most likely to be well-balanced and impartial?

A No.

B So should the best people be poor or should they be of a comfortable class?

A I suppose they should be comfortable.

B Would you expect also that the best people would have the best understanding of the society they are ruling?

A I would expect that, just as you'd want a captain to have a thorough understanding of her ship.

B So the best people, those with the best understanding, should know about the society's history?

A Yes.

B Would you further agree that those who have grown up within the society's oldest institutions would have the best understanding of it?

A That seems right.

B So, given what we've said, would you conclude that the best people to rule a society are those who have attended the oldest schools, been educated at the best universities and come from well-off families?

A I would conclude that.

A I've been wondering what sort of people should rule society.

B Do you think the worst people should rule society?

A Well, no, that's a ridiculous idea.

B So should the best people rule society?

A Yes.

B Would the best people preserve the worst things about society?

A Of course not.

B So the best people would be those who are most capable of correcting the worst things about society?

A Yes, a society has no chance of being the best it can without changing what is worst about it.

B Would you agree that one of the worst aspects of any society is poverty?

A I can't think of anyone who would disagree with that.

B Do you think it's true that to correct something you need to understand it?

A That seems right.

B And who do you think understands poverty more, the rich or the poor?

A The poor, of course.

B Do you also think that the poor would have the most desire to correct poverty?

A Certainly.

B So they would have the most cause to change the worst things about society?

A Yes.

B Are university lecturers poor?

A No, they are quite well-off.

B Would they be able to teach you about poverty?

A I don't think so. Universities are not poor places.

B So are universities the best places to teach you about society?

A It doesn't seem so.

B Would you say that the best people should be those who are most able to make society new?

A Yes, those who can change it and make it better.

B Who would you say is most able to make society new: those who respect the past or those who disrespect it?

A Those who disrespect it, obviously.

B And would you say that those who least respect the past are those who have grown up within society's oldest institutions?

A I wouldn't say that, old institutions don't like change.

B So, given what we've said, would you conclude that the best people to rule a society are those who have not attended the oldest schools or been educated at university, but those who come from poor circumstances and have the least respect for the past?

A I would conclude that.

Appendix 5
Self-Run Sessions

Why not let the class run their own sessions with their own questions? After, say, half a dozen hours, they should have an adequate sense of what philosophy involves. As a prelude you will need to run a session on what makes a session. It should include questions like:

Task Questions 1

❖ What is philosophy?

❖ What are its vital ingredients? What would you have to take out for it not to be philosophy any more?

Task Questions 2

❖ What is a philosophical question?

❖ Is it like a scientific question?

❖ Is it like a mathematical question?

Task Questions 3

❖ What is the role of the teacher?

❖ What shouldn't the teacher do?

With the third question, try to elicit a few basic strategies that the class can use. For example, the teacher:

❖ Asks for reasons – 'Why do you think that?'

❖ Asks for clarity – 'What do you mean by that?'

❖ Links ideas together – 'What do you think of thingy's idea?'

❖ Focuses responses by repeating the question.

And the teacher shouldn't:

- ✦ Interrupt (except to halt an endless talker).
- ✦ Enter into a debate.
- ✦ Evaluate answers.
- ✦ Say what they think.

Give pupils the option of performing in pairs – going solo before the class can be daunting. It's also a good idea to have each person/pair play teacher for just a single question rather than a whole session.

When asking the class to write their own questions, stipulate that they should be closed questions. The questions should be on topics they find interesting, confusing, enraging or exciting. If nothing comes to mind, you can provide a copy of a recent newspaper and ask whether the stories raise any philosophical questions. You can also present question templates, for example:

- ✦ Should we *x*? (e.g. murder murderers, abolish money, eliminate borders, erase bad memories.)
- ✦ Is it wrong to *x*? (e.g. punish, engage in civil disobedience, steal from the rich, invade people's privacy.)
- ✦ Is *x* bad? (e.g. death, hatred, frustration, desire, war, weakness, society.)
- ✦ Do we need *x*? (e.g. education, government, freedom, God, language, other people.)
- ✦ Is it possible to *x*? (e.g. blow up the universe, think of nothing, know everything, end violence.)
- ✦ Are we all *x*? (e.g. oppressed, mortal, equal, fundamentally good, animals.)

With a template such as, 'Do we need *x*?', you can give your pupils a list of abstract nouns and ask them to keep inserting words till they hit on a question that intrigues them. For example, looking online at a list of abstract nouns and confining my search to 'C', I find such questions as: Do we need chaos? Do we need charity? Do we need childhood? Do we need confusion? Do we need crime?

If your class are familiar with abstract nouns, you can build a random question generator, i.e. put their words in a hat and ask a pupil to fish one out. With the penultimate template, 'Is it possible to x?', the generator can be built out of two hats: one for abstract nouns and the other for verbs. This will generate a lot of nonsense and as a task you can investigate whether there's some hidden sense to be made. If, say, you were to arrive at the question, 'Is it possible to kiss time?', this could be rewritten as, 'Is time physical?', which, curiously, is a question of whether 'time' should be in the abstract nouns hat in the first place.

Appendix 6
Basic Logic

Before presenting your class with structured arguments – there are a few within the sessions and a lot in Appendix 7 – you should take them through how arguments fit together and how they can be analysed. Take this example:

1.   If Romeo dies, then Juliet dies.

2.   Romeo dies.

3.   Therefore Juliet dies.

There are two premises and a conclusion. In an argument the conclusion is supposed to logically follow from the premises. You could present this to the class as $1 + 2 = 3$ (where + signifies conjunction rather than addition). The premises are like pillars that support the conclusion. If one is weak, or they do not properly connect to either each other or the conclusion, then the conclusion collapses. So, if you want to reject the conclusion, you need to either destroy one of the premises (show that it is false) or establish that they are poorly connected to each other or the conclusion (show that the reasoning is bad).

An argument is perfect when it's sound. An argument is sound when its premises are true and it is valid. A valid argument is one with good reasoning. If the argument is sound, you must accept its conclusion. In the above example the premises are true, the reasoning is fine – that type of inference (from if p then q, p, therefore q) is called *modus ponens* – and so the argument is sound. The conclusion stands.

It follows, then, that an argument can fail on two counts: 1. the conclusion doesn't logically follow from the premises, or 2. there is a false premise. The first is concerned with the argument's validity. An argument is valid if the conclusion does follow from its premises, i.e. if the premises were true, then the conclusion would be true. For example:

1. Every star is made of snow.

2. The sun is a star.

3. Therefore the sun is made of snow.

This argument is straightforwardly valid; the conclusion follows from the premises. However, the conclusion is false. If the logic is good, but the conclusion bad, that means there is a false premise, which means the argument isn't sound. In this case, premise 1 is false, and the argument's slick logic means that the false premise slides through to a false conclusion. A false premise is enough to sink an argument.

On the other hand, it may be that the premises are true but the reasoning is faulty (a fallacy has been made). Bear in mind that the reasoning can be faulty yet the conclusion true. For example:

1. If Romeo dies, then Juliet dies.

2. Romeo dies.

3. Therefore Paris dies.

As it happens the conclusion is true, but it doesn't logically follow from the premises so the argument is not sound; this means that the argument is not sufficient to prove the conclusion so we are under no obligation to accept it. Let's consider an example where funny reasoning is not as obvious:

1. If it is humid, I will not sleep well.

2. It is not humid.

3. Therefore I will sleep well.

The premises could well be true, but the argument is invalid: the conclusion doesn't follow from the premises. (This fallacious inference is called denying the antecedent: if p then q, not p, therefore not q. Denying the consequent, however, is valid: not p does follow from if p then q, and not q.) There may be other factors besides humidity that prevent me from sleeping well – I may drink too much coffee or there may be a party upstairs. For the argument to be valid, the first premise would have to be: I won't sleep well, if *and only if* it is humid. So, true premises do not guarantee good arguments.

The weak reasoning link doesn't just have to be between the premises and the conclusion, it can occur between the premises. For example:

1. If it is humid, I will not sleep well.

2. But if I do sleep well, I won't be a dope in the morning.

3. It is not humid.

4. Therefore I will sleep well.

5. Therefore I won't be a dope in the morning.

The conclusion does follow from 2 and 4, so the inference to 5 isn't really a problem. Of course, the argument isn't valid, but this is because the faulty reasoning occurs earlier, with the inference from 1 and 3 to 4. When you're looking for bad reasoning, you're looking at how the premises connect together as well as how they connect to the conclusion.

In summary: a good argument is a sound argument – one that is valid with true premises. In order to collapse an argument and undermine the conclusion, you need to find either a false premise or a faulty inference.

Appendix 7
Puzzles

Sessions based on the following so-called puzzles are intended to be more open and improvisatory than those found in the rest of the book. The puzzles are not really puzzles at all; the aim isn't necessarily to solve or refute them – they are more like provocations.

Simply present one to the class and ask whether they accept or reject the conclusion. Allow a talk time in which they can identify where the argument falters, considering which premises are false or which inferences are suspect.

The subsequent discussion may focus on a particular premise, or the conclusion in isolation, or an altogether new idea that spirals from premise to prominence.

1. Only God can create something from nothing.
2. I make my own thoughts.
3. My mind is the sum of my thoughts.
4. Therefore I make my own mind.
5. What am I? My mind.
6. Therefore my mind makes itself.
7. A thing that has made itself has made itself from nothing.
8. Therefore my mind is God.

----

1. I own my mind.
2. If I own the whole of something, then I own the parts of it too.
3. My thoughts are part of my mind.

4.   Therefore I own my thoughts.

5.   I think about you.

6.   Therefore I own thoughts of you.

7.   You are part of those thoughts.

8.   But as 2 states, if I own the whole, I own the parts.

9.   Therefore I own you.

----

1.   Thinking about thinking is like trying to inspect a magnifying glass with itself.

2.   It is impossible to inspect a magnifying glass with itself (i.e. the glass can't magnify itself).

3.   Therefore thinking about thinking is impossible.

4.   Therefore we cannot know what thinking is.

5.   Therefore we can never know whether we are thinking or not.

----

1.   My mind is able to perceive everything in the world.

2.   But my mind cannot perceive itself.

3.   Therefore my mind is not in the world.

----

1.   Before I was born the defining thing about me was that I was nothing.

2.   If we lose a defining aspect of ourselves, then we are no longer ourselves.

3.   Therefore, if I stopped being nothing, I'd stop being myself.

4.   But I am myself.

5. Therefore I am nothing.

After Derrida:

1. Forgiveness is needed to overcome anger.
2. Unforgivable acts cause the most anger.
3. Therefore, unforgivable acts are most in need of forgiveness.
4. But such acts are unforgivable.
5. Therefore the concept of forgiveness is flawed.

---

1. Art is beautiful.
2. If the world were beautiful, we wouldn't need to make art.
3. But we do make art.
4. Therefore the world isn't beautiful.

---

1. If I see myself in a photograph, I say, 'That's me.'
2. If I read the thoughts I've written down, I don't say, 'That's me.'
3. Therefore I am defined by my appearance and not my thoughts.

---

1. The law tells us the truth about what is wrong.
2. The government can change the laws.
3. Therefore the government can change the truth.

---

1. Science constantly changes.

2. Truth is fixed, it never changes.

3. Therefore science isn't true.

----

1. If God is all powerful, He cannot suffer.

2. Since God cannot experience suffering, he cannot sympathise with our suffering.

3. But sympathy is required for love.

4. So either God is not all powerful or He does not love us.

5. If God were not all powerful, there would conceivably be something greater than Him.

6. But there cannot be anything greater than God.

7. Therefore, if there is a God, He does not love us.

----

1. Knowledge is gained from experience.

2. The only life we have fully experienced is our own.

3. Therefore we can only fully know ourselves.

4. But loving others requires knowing them.

5. Therefore we can only fully love ourselves.

From Diogenes:

1. All things belong to the gods.

2. The wise are friends of the gods.

3. Friends share everything.

4. Therefore all things belong to the wise.

----

1. Sharing is good.
2. The best things to share are the best things we have.
3. Children are the best things parents have.
4. Therefore children should be shared.
5. Therefore children should have many parents, not just two.

From Berkeley:

1. When you lie in the sun you feel warm pleasure (you do not feel heat and pleasure separately).
2. Therefore heat is a kind of pleasure.
3. Pleasure cannot exist without being felt.
4. Therefore heat cannot exist without being felt, it is not an objective feature of the world.

----

1. Like the orbits of planets, everything in nature is controlled by laws.
2. My mind is part of nature.
3. Therefore my mind is controlled by laws.
4. Therefore my mind is not free.

----

1. When I step on a nail I feel a pain in my foot.
2. But pain is a mental phenomenon, a feature of the mind.
3. Therefore my mind is in my foot.

----

1. Rules show us how to act in general situations.
2. But every situation is new.
3. Therefore there can be no rules.

   ----

1. Only those who understand your life can tell you what to do.
2. But no one has ever lived your life before, it is entirely new.
3. Therefore no one can really understand your life.
4. Therefore no one can tell you what to do, not even yourself.

   ----

1. Those with the most wealth have the most power.
2. The wealthiest people are among the greediest.
3. Greedy people are bad people.
4. Therefore bad people have the most power.
5. Therefore the people most capable of making society good are not interested in doing so.
6. Therefore society will never be good.

   ----

1. If you want something, then you don't have it.
2. So if you have it, then you don't want it.
3. Therefore we never want what we have.
4. Therefore satisfaction is impossible.

Further Reading

Below is a list of works either referenced or related.

Animals

* J. M. Coetzee, *The Lives of Animals*
* Jonathan Safran Foer, *Eating Animals*
* Plutarch, 'On the Eating of Flesh'
* Ovid, *Metamorphoses*, Book 15

Art and Reality

* Clement Greenberg, 'Modernist Painting', *The Philosophy of Art: Readings Ancient and Modern*

Autonomy

* D. W. Winnicott, 'Ego Distortions in Terms of True Self and False Self', *The Maturational Processes and the Facilitating Environment*
* Faith McNulty, *The Burning Bed*
* Isaiah Berlin, *Four Essays on Liberty*

Belief in God

* William James, *The Will to Believe and Human Immortality*
* Ludwig Wittgenstein, *Lectures and Conversations on Aesthetics, Psychology and Religious Belief*

Conviction

* William James, *Pragmatism*

- Richard Rorty, 'Truth without Correspondence to Reality', *Philosophy and Social Hope*
- Ralph Waldo Emerson, *Essays: Series 1 and 2*

Desire

- ed. Bhikkhu Bodhi, *In the Buddha's Words: An Anthology of Discussions from the Pāli Canon*
- ed. Bhikkhu Bodhi, *The Connected Discourses of the Buddha: A New Translation of Samyutta Nikāya*

Emotions

- Plutarch, *On the Control of Anger*
- Jean-Paul Sartre, *Sketch for a Theory of the Emotions*

Feelings and Rights

- Richard Rorty, 'Human Rights, Rationality, and Sentimentality', *Truth and Progress*
- ed. Shlomo Avineri and Avner de-Shalit, *Communitarianism and Individualism*
- G. E. M. Anscombe, 'Modern Moral Philosophy', *Human Life, Action and Ethics*
- Alasdair MacIntyre, *A Short History of Ethics*

Gender

- Marjorie Garber, *Vested Interests: Cross-Dressing and Cultural Anxiety*
- Marina Warner, *Joan of Arc: The Image of Female Heroism*

Human Omniscience

- ❖ Brian Greene, *The Elegant Universe*
- ❖ Roger Penrose, *The Emperor's New Mind*
- ❖ Colin McGinn, 'Can We Solve the Mind–Body Problem?', *The Nature of Consciousness: Philosophical Debates*

Imperialism and Magic

- ❖ James Frazer, *The Golden Bough*
- ❖ E. E. Evans-Pritchard, *Witchcraft, Oracles and Magic among the Azande*
- ❖ Peter Winch, 'Understanding a Primitive Society', *Ethics and Action*

Language and Originality

- ❖ Richard Poirier, *The Renewal of Literature: Emersonian Reflections*
- ❖ W. H. Auden, 'D. H. Lawrence', *The Dyer's Hand*
- ❖ D. H. Lawrence, 'Whitman', *Selected Essays*
- ❖ Morse Peckham, *Man's Rage for Chaos*

Lying

- ❖ Oscar Wilde, 'The Decay of Lying', *The Decay of Lying: And Other Essays*
- ❖ St Augustine, *De Mendacio*

Madness

- ❖ Eric Fromm, *The Sane Society*
- ❖ R. D. Laing, *The Divided Self*
- ❖ Adam Phillips, *Going Sane*

- ❖ Maurice O'Connor Drury, 'Madness and Religion', *The Danger of Words*

Mind and Body

- ❖ Plato, *Phaedo*
- ❖ Plotinus, *The Enneads*
- ❖ Elizabeth V. Spelman, 'Woman as Body: Ancient and Contemporary Views', *Feminist Theory and the Body: A Reader*
- ❖ Ludwig Wittgenstein, *Philosophical Investigations*
- ❖ Andrew Marvell, 'A Dialogue between the Soul and Body'

Money

- ❖ Marx and Engels, *The Communist Manifesto*
- ❖ G. A. Cohen, *If You're an Egalitarian, How Come You're So Rich?*

Morality and the Law

- ❖ Henry David Thoreau, *Civil Disobedience*

The Nature of Evil

- ❖ Hannah Arendt, *Eichmann in Jerusalem: A Report on the Banality of Evil*
- ❖ Jacqueline Rose, 'The Body of Evil: Arendt, Coetzee, and 9/11', *The Jacqueline Rose Reader*

Newness

- ❖ Robert Macfarlane, *Original Copy: Plagiarism and Originality in Nineteenth-Century Literature*

- Christine Battersby, *Gender and Genius: Towards a Feminist Aesthetics*
- David Shields, *Reality Hunger: A Manifesto*

Objects and Essences

- ed. Richard Rorty, *The Linguistic Turn: Essays in Philosophical Method*
- A. J. Ayer, *Language, Truth and Logic*
- Ludwig Wittgenstein, *Tractatus Logico-Philosophicus*

Perfectibility

- John Gray, *The Silence of Animals: On Progress and other Modern Myths*

Power

- Plato, *The Republic*
- William Godwin, *An Enquiry Concerning Political Justice*

Privacy

- Ludwig Wittgenstein, *Philosophical Investigations*

Race

- Karen and Barbara Fields, *Racecraft: The Soul of Inequality in American Life*
- Ashley Montagu, *Man's Most Dangerous Myth: The Fallacy of Race*

Responsibility

- Simone de Beauvoir, *The Ethics of Ambiguity*

❖ Jean-Paul Sartre, *Existentialism and Humanism*

Scepticism

❖ G. E. Moore, 'Proof of an External World', *Epistemology: An Anthology,* ed. Ernest Sosa, Jaegwon Kim, Jeremy Fantl and Matthew McGrath

❖ René Descartes, *Meditations on First Philosophy*

❖ Stanley Cavell, *The Claim of Reason*

❖ Ludwig Wittgenstein, *On Certainty*

The Senses

❖ Aldous Huxley, *The Doors of Perception*

❖ Wassily Kandinsky, *Concerning the Spiritual in Art*

❖ Jacques Derrida, *Memoirs of the Blind: The Self-Portrait and Other Ruins*

❖ Helen Keller, *The Story of My Life*

❖ Oliver Sacks, 'The Disembodied Lady', *The Man who Mistook His Wife for a Hat*

Sin

❖ St Augustine, *Confessions*

The Soul

❖ Paul Churchland, 'Eliminative Materialism and the Propositional Attitudes', *Philosophy of Mind: Contemporary Readings*

Street Art

❖ Dave Hickey, *The Invisible Dragon: Four Essays on Beauty*

❖ Dave Hickey, *Air Guitar: Essays on Art and Democracy*

Suicide

❖ Plato, *Phaedo*

❖ St Augustine, *The City of God*

❖ Cicero, 'On Duties'

❖ Seneca, 'On Providence'

❖ Al Avarez, *The Savage God*

Temptation

❖ Friedrich Nietzsche, *On the Genealogy of Morality*

❖ Sigmund Freud, *Civilization and its Discontents*

❖ Jean-Jacques Rousseau, *Emile*

Thinking

❖ D. T. Suzuki, *The Zen Doctrine of No-Mind*

❖ Hannah Arendt, *The Life of the Mind: Thinking, Vol. 1*

Time

❖ William Hazlitt, 'On the Past and Future', *Table-Talk: Essays on Men and Manners*

Torture

❖ Adam Smith, *The Theory of Moral Sentiments*

❖ Jean Améry, 'Torture', *At the Mind's Limits: Contemplations by a Survivor on Auschwitz and its Realities*

❖ J. M. Coetzee, 'The Problem of Evil', *Elizabeth Costello*

Tradition and Change

* Edmund Burke, *Reflections on the Revolution in France*
* Edmund Burke, *Letters on a Regicide Peace*
* Thomas Carlyle, *The French Revolution*
* Albert Soboul, *The Sans-Culotte: The Popular Movement and Revolutionary Government, 1793–1794*

Understanding Death

* Sigmund Freud, *Beyond the Pleasure Principle*
* Martin Heidegger, *Being and Time*
* Albert Camus, *The Myth of Sisyphus*

Utopia

* William Morris, *News from Nowhere*
* Francis Bacon, *New Atlantis*
* H. G. Wells, *Anticipations*

The Philosophy Shop

Ideas, Activities and Questions to Get People, Young and Old, Thinking Philosophically

Edited by Peter Worley

ISBN: 978-178135264-9

The Philosophy Shop is a veritable emporium of philosophical puzzles and challenges to develop thinking in and out of the classroom.

Thoughtings

Puzzles, Problems and Paradoxes in Poetry to Think With

Peter Worley and Andrew Day

ISBN: 978-178135087-4

These are not poems or, at least, not in the traditional sense of the word … They are a kind of poem specifically designed around a particular puzzle or problem that might be thought more philosophy than poetry.

- Type up provocation.
- Do CVs for day camps & put them on netl website.
- Ask Naddy & do Morpeth & BMI posters
- Ironing
- Books for next few weeks. (& records)
- CPH & GMG dates.
- Do not newsletter
- Resources for Bilston, Penzance, Dillington & Higham
- Stoic retreats promo email
- Marketing plan for July